Communication in Marriage

How to Reconnect With Your Spouse, Resolve Conflict and Create a Loving and Healthy Relationship

Amber Wise

Table of Contents

Introduction

An intimate relationship is a close bond between two parties, in which the couple shares their feelings and thoughts while spending their lives together in any manner that reinforces the tie. However, relationships can never be formed for certain individuals who associate them with unpleasant emotions, such as stress, frustration, and fear, after being attached to someone for a certain period of time. It is undeniably normal for marital disputes to surface in the later stage of a relationship. These conflicts are frequently caused by an argument or unhappiness between the two parties. As a consequence, the situation within the relationship will end up in insecurity and ultimately lead to a negative outcome.

The vital elements of any relationship are trust and mutual understanding, it doesn't matter how deeply in love they are or were. If there is fear, one party can feel paranoid that the other party is being unfaithful or is not interested.

If this situation is prolonged, it will aggravate the level of anxiety and possibly lead to the negative intuitions. If you encounter this, you should take the first step to reconcile the lack of confidence in your relationship with your partner. Seek to resolve your current fear by respectfully disclosing your feelings of mistrust to your partner and digging down to the source of feeling worried. It is strongly recommended that all parties interact with frankness to recognize and understand the root causes of a distressed relationship.

Spending time together or taking part in any joint activities will help to strengthen the bond. Going together for a vacation, for example, and enjoying a wonderful place will allow both parties to create unforgettable memories while staying away from their usual stressful urban life.

In a relationship, one needs to learn to forgive, accept, and negotiate. Controversy over an issue will not be beneficial to either party. It will only cause more frustration or fear, which will inevitably deteriorate. Do not indulge in any inappropriate acts or words that may injure your loved one. Furthermore, step back a little by tolerating him/her, just for the simple reason that it brings you to the wonderful feeling you had when you had first met. If you could do this, the anxiety in your relationship will eventually cease.

Appreciation is another important factor in handling frustration and fear in a relationship. Often making a rash decision, or moving too fast to a conclusion, won't help you find the answer. Anxiety at the onset of a horrific incident may be frightening. Learn to relax by taking a deep breath and refreshing your memory on the things you both used to do together. Think how amazing is the ultimate bond that brought you both together. Intimate greetings and body gestures will also help you to show your partner that you care about him/her and will also help you express your feelings more implicitly. Having been through the process, you will realize one day that each of you will begin to respect each other naturally, even without the intervention of any "mechanism."

Moreover, good communication is one of the most valuable lessons we all learn in life. For a successful marriage, it goes hand in hand with a good one. This is the secret to maintaining a happy marriage. Good communication means that when you communicate, you both understand each other. The faster you know how to communicate with your partner, the better the marriage. Why? Communication issues are the key reasons, or root causes, of the top issues that end in divorce, splitting up, or breeding dysfunctional relationships among married couples.

Communication is important to everything you do in your marriage and with your partner. The desire and willingness of you and your spouse are required to enhance communication within the marriage. An intentional effort will be expected from you and your partner to interact in a better manner in your marriage. Through learning how to interact effectively with your partner, you can thrive in your marriage, do things you never thought possible, and excel in all the various areas of your life.

Chapter 1:
Importance of Communication for a Couple

Why is Communication Important in Relationships? Imagine a world where the concept of language and talking does not exist. The quiet may seem alluring, but do not be fooled! Do you realize how infuriating the mere process of giving directions would be? How would it feel to be unable to describe the beauty of colors or nature anymore? Would it not feel suffocating to be unable to sing or express your love, admiration, or gratitude?

A relationship is no different. It is like a driver that needs direction to reach the desired location. It is a child who needs to be taught what is wrong and right so he can choose the right path and not go astray. It is like a student who needs validation for his work to make him feel appreciated. A relationship needs communication, just as a fish needs water. Relationships are like precious, soft putty that has been entrusted into your hands, and it is up to you to mold it as per your desire. But, of course, relationships are not molded by skilled hands but skilled hearts. Their nature and fate are decided by what we communicate. Want your partner to be more expressive? Tell them! Does your partner feel like you need to be tidier? Hear them out!

To summarize, communication is VERY important for any relationship. In fact, the level of communication defines the strength and longevity of a relationship. So, while you are busy showering your loved one with gifts, make sure you do not neglect to lay down bricks for the bridge of communication!

How Does Communication Affect Relationships?

To put it simply, the answer is A LOT of ways. It is highly understandable how something as vital as communication would affect relationships in multiple ways. If you are still questioning whether the effort to bring communication into your relationship will be worth it or not, then give these following reasons a read and let your spirits soar high.

- **It makes both individuals feel appreciated**. Validation and affection are basic human needs. No one likes feeling unappreciated or neglected, especially within a relationship. Communication is not just a system that allows you to express what is wrong. This habit of letting the other one know how you feel also transcends into appreciating and valuing your partner when they do something right. Thus, communication ensures that the efforts of both individuals in a relationship never go unnoticed. This creates a positive feedback mechanism by encouraging the parties in a relationship to continue working towards the betterment of their relationship.

- **Communication is poisonous for miscommunications** Imagine this; you send a long and detailed text proclaiming your love for your partner, and all you get in response is a plain, "okay." Would you feel rejected? Hurt? Angry? While "okay" is indeed an unsuitable reply in this case, a strong relationship based on open communication ensures that you do not jump to conclusions. Instead of getting angry, you wonder if all is well with your partner. Instead of accusing them of being heartless, you calmly ask them the reason for such a curt reply. This ability to remain calm and not jump to conclusions can only be achieved once you know how the other individual generally communicates.

- **Your relationship does not have room for arguments**.

Arguments are often based on a misunderstanding or a fight for dominance. Communication allows you to be honest and trusting of each other. Thus, when a disagreement arises, you two approach it as a discussion. Think of it as a case of you two versus the problem as opposed to you two against each other. Good communication serves as a safe haven to express how you feel without fear of judgment or repercussion. Thus, your relationship does not feel the need to argue anymore.

- **You feel intimate with your partner**. Relationships are not just defined by titles and dates. The intimacy of a relationship is judged by how well you two know each other and the connection you share. This emotional connection and feeling of intimacy can only be fostered once you two are willing to be vulnerable and open. This is accomplished by communicating with your partner and making your partner feel heard. Therefore, by improving the communication in your relationship, you will be bringing your partner much closer to yourself and discovering things about them that you never ever noticed before.

- **You always have context**. A lack of communication often breeds insecurity and jealousy. When you lack information about the emotional state of your other half, you constantly tend to jump to conclusions. This attitude is not only damaging to your mental health but it can also become suffocating or claustrophobic for your partner. However, good and strong communication with each other helps you understand the context in reference to which the other person has mentioned something. This helps you understand the need to give each other breathing space when required.

• **It prevents unpleasant surprises**. Imagine devoting ten years of your life to someone only to find out that they do not share your views on children. How would you feel if your partner's lifestyle choices are in stark contrast to yours? Would you really have the right to be angry at your better half if you have never even expressed what angers you? Getting serious about a relationship without having communicated properly is akin to buying a mystery box. You never know what it might reveal! By communicating, you let the other one know about your expectations and how you feel about certain things.

• **Communication helps establish trust**. We have seen how communication helps establish intimacy, it provides context for each other's actions, and, most importantly, it helps avoid fights and misunderstandings. Communication gives you the key to create a strong foundation for your relationship, and that is "mutual trust." Your partner should feel appreciated and understood. This helps them trust you and your love, allowing them to see you as a safe haven where they can be vulnerable without inhibition. Mutual trust saves you from a lot of stress, as you can always feel free to ask your partner for the reason for their unlikely actions rather than making assumptions.

In conclusion, communication is a magical box just waiting to be opened, so it can shower you with myriads of gifts, ranging from intimacy to understanding and eventually forming a strong everlasting bond. A bond strengthened by communication is stronger than steel and can withstand any test of time. Thus, make sure to communicate so you can develop the relationship you have always dreamed of.

The Effects of Loneliness

Being lonely warps the mind and does physical harm to the body. A neurological study conducted on the brain's response to rejection and isolation found that the emotional pain experienced by the outsider resulted in negative physical symptoms through the anterior cingulate cortex of the brain. Loneliness results in higher stress and a lowered immune system. You can actually get sick from being a loner!

Make no mistake, experiencing loneliness does not mean literally being alone. Married couples can feel loneliness despite sharing a house together. According to John Cacioppo, a neuroscientist and psychologist at the University of Chicago, something as simple as being busy with work keeps you from connecting with your partner and creates a feeling of isolation.

The same can happen if you and your mister or missus feel bored in the relationship. When nothing provides exciting stimuli, you turn to yourself and your own thoughts for entertainment. Instead, you will find yourself going over your flaws because you are faced with that ugly internal mirror we call self-doubt. Humans have trouble dealing with that so much that we create a phantom presence to cope.

Believe it or not, that is how a belief in the supernatural flourishes. This is largely due to the lack of the secondary information and solidity that comes with a pack of people upon whom you may rely to confirm or deny your own experiences. Every unfamiliar sound we process becomes uncertain and leaves open the possibility of phantasms, the logic here being that we did not create the noise, so who did? That is why it is supremely beneficial to spend time with your partner regularly. You will legitimately go crazy if you do not!

The Life Saving Benefits of Communication

The reason that partner-to-partner communication is so vital is that this person gives you another perspective and a way of impartially viewing a situation. A partner can remind you that keeping your job means keeping a house and food and that you are still advancing your career even if your boss is a jerk.

Your special someone teaches you wisdom throughout your life. That said, not communicating with your partner before making big decisions may lead to your ruin. The burden of stress falls on them to keep providing support while you search for an alternative. You fight more and may ultimately split. I assume you are reading this to stay together, so here is what you should do to avoid heartbreak.

Make time to sit down together and rationally discuss big changes. Come to a compromise and work toward your common interests. You will not only save your relationship, but you will strengthen the ties that bind you.

The Physical over the Digital

Fights can start just because something you said was taken the wrong way over SMS. Since your partner cannot hear the tone of your voice, they have to assume the way you felt. Just the tiniest bit of insecurity will lead to an automatic conclusion that you were negative.

Relationships thrive on physical touch and intimacy. Remember before when I mentioned the negative side-effects that come from loneliness? Not being touched for long periods of time contribute to it. Here are a few tips to get that romantic spark and increase in positive communication back in your love life. Aside from the obvious sexual nature of physical affection, there are little things you can do to keep loneliness at bay and fall in love again.

1. Offer to give your partner a massage after a long and stressful day. They will appreciate the effort you show to help them relax.

2. Lightly caress a shoulder as you pass by to let your lover know that you are thinking of them, even when you are not sitting down and experiencing something together.

3. Hug them regularly. Hugs provide a sense of security and warmth. Ultimately, it creates a deep bond of trust.

Chapter 2:
Importance of Communication

When it comes to a couple's life, communication is vital. It is a beautiful thing, but it isn't going to be without trouble. Daily life, finances, stress, work, kids, and other items all come up, and the two of you can't work as a team if there isn't an open line of productive and loving communication.

Communication Will Build Strong Bonds

It is not enough for just one partner to come to the table and do all of the communication. Both sides need to be able and willing to express themselves and communicate with the other party.

It isn't a secret that couples who can communicate well with have happier and longer relationships. This goes the other way as well. Those couples who barely connect at all, who find communication to be a chore or boring, or who hardly take time for each other and focus on one another are unlikely to keep their relationship going, at least until some significant change happen.

It isn't enough to communicate upon occasion. Setting up a monthly meeting to speak for an hour and then not talking to each other will not cut it for the rest of the month. Constant communication will develop stronger bonds. It allows the couple to learn more about one another, become better equipped to handle problems, and share their best life experiences. But this only works if they continuously work to keep an open line of communication with each other.

Communication Can Help Prevent Wrong Assumptions, Confusions, and Misunderstandings

When looking through the context of any couples' life, keeping things unresolved can lead to many problems along the way. Arguments can end up getting out of hand quickly, marital matters become exploded and taken out of context, and things that were supposed to be non-issues become the trigger for some significant conflicts.

You will be surprised at how many of the above issues can be resolved if the couple just learns how to reach out to one another and communicate more effectively.

Communication Can Keep the Couples Connected on an Emotional Level

If you want to make sure that your togetherness is going to last your whole life, you need to maintain an emotional connection with your partner. Healthy communication can help with this.

It is no secret that healthy and constant communication is one of the essential ingredient in helping couples stay emotionally invested in each other and their union. Those couples who are able to maintain a constant level of contact with each other often create and share happier memories, share more of their experiences together, and are actually quite a bit happier with one another in general.

Marital States

You will find out that all kinds of things potentially cause an issue within couples. While there are different options you can choose to prevent and resolve the conflicts that come up in a couple's life, communication is the best and most powerful of all.

In addition to the idea that communication can help correct different issues, it also helps prevent some of these problems from even showing up in the first place. When a couple can talk about their concerns and any issues they have effectively, they will find solutions ahead of time. They can also prevent these issues from compromising their relationship later on.

What does it take to make a relationship work?

It is a fact that we know all too well. Not all relationships are going to last, and this is a sad statistic to focus on. Of course, you want to make sure that yours lasts. You want to stay committed and near the other person. They are your soulmate, the best person for you, and your better half. For the unions that have lasted, there are a few secrets that made things work out for them. Of course, there isn't one element that all on its own did it. Rather, any relationship's success will depend on many different factors, all of which work hand in hand. These help couples stay together, even in a world where many problems and hardships can arise. Some of the most significant factors that help determine if a relationship is going to last or not include:

• **Mutual respect**. Respect is going to be a foundational element in any kind of relationship. Both partners must respect each other when it comes to all matters. This doesn't mean that you have to go along and agree with the other person, and it doesn't mean that you always have to give in. But it does mean that if you do have a thing that brings up displeasure with your partner, you find the proper and respectful way to express yourself.

It would help if you aimed never to show your partner disrespect. A constant showing of disrespect not only shows a big red flag for your relationship, but it could also be a sign of a personality issue in the individual who indicates that behavior.

• **Knowing how to handle any problems in the proper manner**. Every couple is going to run into their issues. And even a perfect-looking relationship is going to run into issues at some times. But the way the two in the association choose to handle these issues will help separate the dysfunctional union from the functional ones.

When a couple has agreed to stay together and work through things no matter what, they will sit down together and look for solutions calmly. Both sides get to say their piece and let their feelings be known before they have to make any decisions. The partners are also going to consider how the other one feels before they make any choices. And finally, those in one of these healthy relationships know that their alliance is so much bigger than the everyday issues present themselves.

• **Embrace any imperfections**. There isn't such a thing as a perfect couple. If this is the idea that you have about the relationship in your head, then now is the time to make some changes and start to understand that all couples will run into problems at one point or another. Your partner is always going to have their flaws, and you will too. It is up to you to accept these and never allow them to tear the relationship apart.

Beyond acceptance, the person needs to see still if they can fix any of the flaws. This doesn't mean that you have to go through hell and change everything about you. But if your partners complain that you are putting the clothes next to the laundry basket instead of inside it, you can work on that one and others like it.

• **Put the relationship as a top priority**. When you are in a relationship, you and your partner enter into a contract that says you both will stay together, no matter what. While technically, you can go through divorce or separation as an option, a functional couple understands that they need to avoid those two things and try to make their relationship work at all costs.

To ensure that any relationship is going to work, both sides need to prioritize the relationship. Both sides have to make the necessary steps to provide for the association, give their partner some time, work in an effective way to resolve any conflicts that come up. When you and your partner take the time to prioritize your relationship, everything else, from the expenses to your children and so on, will start to fall into place naturally.

• **It takes constant effort to make things work**. It is not always easy to make a couple's life work. It will take a lot of patience, compassion, passion, effort, and time to make the relationship work. Just because you signed the piece of paper and had that big ceremony or done in a secret room for courtship, as the case may be, doesn't mean that you are all done with the work. And with so many problems and responsibilities you will need to face throughout your life as a couple, it is so crucial that both sides of every relationship make all the effort they can to make the courtship or relationship work.

You will quickly find that the relationship will not last if only one side tries to solve the problems and if one side shows affection. One side could be performing all the responsibilities. Even when you were in the courtship phase with your partner, the romantic relationship was meant to be a two-way street.

Open communication is the heart of the matter to make any relationship work. A relationship is a life-long commitment, and it is going to take some time and effort to see results.

Signs of Poor Communication in a Relationship

In every relationship, we all understand the value of good communication. Lack of contact or mismanagement has destroyed so many relationships. Many relationships failed, and the poor communication forced many couples to split up. Healthy contact is important for sustaining a marriage or other romantic relationship.

Communication is not only a topic of debate. Good communication requires versatility, consideration, affection, and selflessness to promote successful relationships.

The conversation between you two may rarely go deeper than the surface. In the early days of a relationship, partners usually talk a lot about each other to know more about each other. Yet this appears to slow down and fade over time. When you feel this in your relationship, you have to fix it. So how?

If you don't ask each other about their day, asking for this demonstrates interest and gives you a starting point for a discussion. If none of you bothers asking, then it is a serious matter that needs to be addressed. You just want to think more about your agenda and not ready to listen to the other person's question.

One or both of you has surely more often lost control and got frustrated quite quickly. Now the majority of the interactions were about nagging.

When you are disturbed by something, and you presume things, you leap to conclusions rather than talking it out. It leads the relationship to a breakup. Your relationship needs serious focus a big leap in communication.

Don't always think that you know your partner well and constantly respond on the basis of past behavior. If you both stop the personal hot buttons, it is a sign of unresolved problems and a lack of mutual confidence.

Miscommunication or no communication at all adversely affects a relationship. To get the relationship working again, communication issues need to be addressed.

Here is a list of ideas that can be applied to a relationship to overcome communication problems:

Tell your partner, "How are you?" and "how was your day? Initiating a positive, conversational vibe shows you love and care.

Seek to spend more time with each other. Go for lunch or dinner or schedule a vacation somewhere and try to get to know each other's thoughts and points of view on different things. Address the difficult moments and remember each other's happy days.

Never take something on yourself about your partner without knowing the truth. Making assumption and trying to read your partner's mind frequently contribute to misunderstandings and hurt feelings.

When your friend/partner is talking to you, listen carefully and with relaxed eye contact. If your partner needs you somewhere, react positively to them. Don't nitpick; tell them if you have any problem.

It will corrode your friendship if you don't.

Have a daily partnership check-in and talk about your shared decision and also about your relationship.

Believing in life will change things. Display your optimistic attitude about problems and your relationship during contact.

Speak to your friend about things before they happen, like any family-related problem that you expect or any difficult job situation.

Say thank you every time your partner helps you with something. Appreciate their little movements or behaviors that they are doing to satisfy you.

If you are upset by something, explain yourself and make your partner understand what you mean and how it affects you. When you have to speak to your partner about something they do not like, choose a convenient time to do so. If your partner is distracted or in a rush, or in pain, do not discuss something.

Take the time to make things you enjoy about each other complement one another.

Now, if you believe something in your relationship is lacking, then go to your partner and speak up. Share your feelings and discuss whatever you want to communicate; this will make your relationship safe and solid.

Chapter 3:
Verbal and Nonverbal Communication

Nonverbal Communication

For this discussion, nonverbal communication is akin to body language. Let us start with facial expressions that affirm that the human face is highly expressive and communicates countless emotions without vocalizing anything. A great aspect of nonverbal communication is that it is largely standard as the facial expression for anger, happiness, and fear is similar across different cultures. Like most aspects of nonverbal communication, one has little control over the source and manifestation of facial expression, making it a critical aspect of evaluating the honesty of communication. From facial expressions, we can determine how one is feeling.

Beginning with body movement and posture, how one stands, sits, holds their head, or walks affect how others perceive one. For instance, your posture communicates much about your attentiveness and eagerness when listening to a speech. Your posture also communicates your emotional status. If one is angry, he or she is unlikely to appear composed and likely to stand upright for long or slouch for long. On the other hand, if one is excited, he or she is likely to change posture and movements frequently than when one feels sad. You must have felt highly excited at one point; you probably walked fast, jumped, sat, and stood up frequently.

Additionally, gestures are the other form of nonverbal communication. Focusing on hand gestures, they are used to beckon, wave, point, or direct. In most cases, hand gestures happen without much intervention from the conscious mind. The meaning of most hand gestures varies across cultures. An innocent message created by a hand gesture in one country may be offensive in another country. One can read the emotional states of a person from hand gestures even if they speak the contrary. For example, when one is angry, he or she is likely to throw their hands in the air in an uncoordinated manner. In most cases, hand gestures contradict verbal communication, especially where one feels emotional and tries to hide it.

Relatedly, there is eye contact that is an important aspect of body language. The way one looks at another person when communicating reveals hostility, affection, interest, and confidence. Individuals that have difficulties initiating and sustaining eye contact are largely considered shy. When an individual feels embarrassed, he or she is likely not to make and sustain eye contact. Sustained eye contact at a particular person or group of people is a stare and indicates judgment. Think of how your instructor looked at you when you were talking while others were writing. Prolonged eye contact is associated with intimidation and judging.

For touch as a component of body language, it evokes significant meaning' and, in some cases, touch influences the development of a person. In the formative years, children need touch, reassuring fondle for them to feel secure and loved. Psychologists can suspect bonding issues where one of the parents shows reluctance to touch and stroke their kid. For adults, touch is expressed commonly as a handshake and a hug. A firm handshake indicates confidence and familiarity, while a weak handshake suggests a lack of confidence and unfamiliarity. A hug serves the same role as a handshake, but hugs for individuals in love may be prolonged.

Equally important, space is part of nonverbal communication. Getting too close to the person you have communication with will make them feel uncomfortable unless it is in an exceptional situation. For lovers trying to connect more, moving closer to each other may sound romantic. In teaching, there is what is called the professional distance, or the standard distance allowable between a teacher and the student when communicating. When someone gets too close, then the other person may feel suffocated, trapped, and intimidated. Getting too far is also counterproductive as it makes the other person strain to participate in the communication.

Correspondingly, the voice is part of nonverbal communication. How loud we speak communicates an emphasis. The pace by which we speak captures our emotional status. If one speaks fast, it may indicate that one has panic or feels insecure and wants to get through with speaking as fast as possible. The tone and inflection of the voice tell more about the attitude of the speaker and the nature of the message. For instance, the message may sound standard and devoid of emotions, but the tone and pitch of the speaker may bring out excitement or temper. The tone of the speaker may indicate sarcasm or anger.

While nonverbal communication can be manipulated or rehearsed, it is difficult to manipulate all forms of nonverbal communication in one instance. It is difficult to rehearse tone, gestures, touch, distance, and facial expressions to align with verbal communication. For this reason, body language remains a reliable source of reading and ascertaining an individual's emotional status. However, it is possible to learn and exert control over your body language to enhance particular outcomes. Just as if we learn to focus our emotions and subsequent reactions, we can exert more control over our body language. There is also a possibility of receiving confusing nonverbal communication that is unintentionally sent by the source. In most cases, confusing nonverbal communication harms relationships. You might have smiled unintentionally, only for your friend to think you are rejoicing that they are suffering.

Against this backdrop, all these smart and well-intentioned people struggle to socialize with others. The unfortunate thing is that they are unaware of the body language they communicate. If one wants to communicate effectively, they should avoid misunderstandings and enjoy a trusting relationship, both professionally and socially. One should understand how to use and interpret body language and enhance their nonverbal communication.

One of the most challenging and most valuable aspects of nonverbal communication is that it is happening even when one is not initiating it. For this reason, body language can be frustrating, especially where one tries to hide something while the body language keeps giving it away. At some point, you have been in a relationship and detected lies from your partner despite the best attempts by your partner to cover their trials. On the other hand, nonverbal communication is the most dependable indicator of an individual's status, even when the person is attempting to mask their true status.

Relatedly, most people feel frustrated by nonverbal communication because they cannot always control it, even with rehearsals. Think of trying to assure your partner that you are not offended, but the tone and pitch of your voice suggest that you are upset. The listener will feel that you are not honest with yourself and with them. It is important to match verbal communication with nonverbal communication and not the other way around. The inability to manifest the desired body language can be a source of distress.

If reading body language, pay attention to inconsistencies exhibited by the communicator. Usually, nonverbal communication should support or amplify verbal communication. Where inconsistencies manifest, then the individual is trying to mask their true emotional status. It is important to analyze nonverbal communication signals as a group rather than a single nonverbal cue. For instance, analyze the tone of voice, hand gestures, facial expressions, and eye contact as a group of related components. Some people are born with conditions that appear to show inconsistencies when communicating nonverbally, but they are honest in their communication.

For instance, they are people born shy due to parental issues that make them reluctant to interact with people. A shy individual will have challenges initiating and sustaining eye contact, which has nothing to do with their emotional status and honesty of their verbal message. There are also persons born with hyperhidrosis, a condition that makes them sweat excessively even when the weather is cold and with no strenuous movement. The hands and feet of such people sweat, and they avoid handshakes or eye contact, which should not be interpreted as panicking, insecurity, and anxiety.

Verbal Communication

Communication systems employ signs and symbols for interaction purposes. Signs are signals used to convey a message, according to the general philosophy of verbal communication. You come to understand a particular signal because you understand the cause of the action. For example, if your child mutters some words and points directly at the door, what does that mean? It means that probably someone is at the door or attention is needed. On the other hand, symbols are marks or words indicating a complex level of reasoning and understanding between the parties involved. Symbols, as complex as they seem, stem from the concept of symbolic interactionism theory.

Whenever verbal communication takes place, we need to understand the symbolic content of what the speaker is talking about. This process is sub-divided into:

<u>Semanticists:</u> semanticists know the relationship between the after-effect of action and what had caused it. Signals stand for a particular meaning even though they might be misconstrued to mean other unrelated things. For example, a little child shouting at the top of his voice with a sharp knife in his hand connotes something definite. You may, however, see such an occurrence differently in terms of the intended message.

<u>Generativity</u>: Generativity takes the stand that a finite message could take the shape of infinite meanings. Communication symbols range from individual to individual. That's why languages are capable of combining and recombining symbols and signals to produce meaningful and comprehensible utterances to the users of the language.

<u>Displacement</u>: this pertains to communicating what is abstract. This is because a language gives room for the communication of things that exist only in the mind. The displacement factor allow for discussing that which only exists in the imagination.

Chapter 4:
Things that Couples Commonly Fight About

Every relationship is different. There are things that couple X fights over while couple Y wouldn't. Fight vary from one couple to the next, but certain factors are common triggers.

Money

People don't like to joke about their money. If one partner turns into a parasite in a marriage, you can be sure that the marriage is doomed. It's not uncommon to see a fistfight over money. The couple is just trying to follow up on their money decisions, but they can become desperate if none of the answers is satisfactory. Unless a couple has invested in a lot of trust between them, it is far better if both persons managed their money.

Lack of Communication

If one party feels as though the family isn't communicating enough, it can be a potential cause for fights. A lack of communication means that the family members are ignoring and may be too busy to talk things over. This habit sows a seed bitterness between the family members. There are usually unresolved issues. The more time passes before the problems are resolved, the worse the wound becomes, and soon all hope of recovery is lost. Couples must improve their communication capabilities if they are lacking.

Sex

This issue not only makes couples fight, but it can even cause bitter breakups. When it comes to sex problems, usually one person feels as though they are being used. One of them wants too much of it while the other isn't comfortable supplying it. Thus the sex-hungry person starts chasing the resistant person, and it creates all manner of conflict as they try to fend him off. Competition can also crop up when a person feels like the other person doesn't participate enough and enjoys sex. They may complain about the lack of enthusiasm on their partner's part, a lack of hygiene, and general clumsiness.

Children

Couples start fighting about children even before they have been born. They may fight about whether they should have children or not in the first place. Then they may fight about when to have them and how many. If a couple wants to adopt, they may fight over the route they intend to take, and if a couple has problems with a natural pregnancy, they might fight over which treatment options to seek. If there was conflict even before the child was born, imagine what it will be like after the birth. Couples often fight over the style of raising their kids. Maybe one person proposes an authoritarian approach, but the one wants a laidback style. They fight over which schools to take their kids to, and it never ends.

Spending Time

Instead of getting together and having a great time, a positive moment can quickly turn into a conflict. First off, the couple may differ on how to spend their time, with one person wanting to do a particular activity while the other wants to do a different one. One partner might be too engrossed on their phone, leaving the other frustrated needy and frustrated. Sometimes a partner will want some alone time after spending time with their partner, causing the other person to be frustrated if it is not a mutual decision. If couples want to avoid conflict about spending time, they have to discuss the specifics and their respective needs.

Romance

Some people get into marriage with lofty dreams and fantasies. But as time passes, reality gives them a harsh jolt. They realize that all the great things they imagined the world owed them were a mirage. In the beginning, there is a lot of romance. But now there's none. Life has become much too routine, and the other person doesn't have the energy to be romantic. If not addressed, this can cause serious rifts in the marriage. Romance keeps partners yearning for one another.

Chores

If one person feels they have become the slave of the house, expect some resistance. They will complain that they never signed up for all the housework by themselves while their partner finds creative ways to sneak away from their responsibilities. One person might always takes the trash out because their partner is a master of excuses. One person might have high cleanliness standards, whereas the other party might have shallow cleanliness habits. This causes tremendous problems as one person feels that the other is having it easy while they slave away.

In-laws

It's not uncommon for one person's family to be against the other person's family. They feel as though their son or daughter isn't a good match. This naturally invites tension and distrust. During fights, one person might disparage the other person's parents, causing the other person to be offended and then return the insult. As with most chronic issues, it never ends.

How to Handle Fights

Fights in a marriage are regular. But it's the way you handle conflicts that makes the difference. Once you understand each other, the arguments become less frequent, and then they disappear altogether.

• Know your true feelings

It's so easy for your partner's reactions to disrupt your emotional state. Always be aware of what certain situations make you feel. This will help you know what's truly important in your life. Mastering your emotions is essential as it will help you fight for your life goals.

• Look at your contribution

It's so easy to shift all the blame onto our partners. But if we are honest with ourselves, we play a huge role in triggering fights. We should learn to see how our words or actions contribute to the messy battle we are in. It takes introspection and self-awareness to be able to identify our role in creating conflict.

• Compromise

Most arguments can be remedied by reaching a compromise. But the problem is that we are egotistical. It's either our way or the highway. Nobody relents and the fighting carries on. If only we were humble enough to seek compromise, our marriages would be a lot more stable.

• Taking breaks

You and your partner just had an epic showdown of name-calling and tearing each other down, so now what? Go off in separate directions and cool off. You can engage in reconciliatory talks when the anger ebbs. But if you keep near each other while the offense is still in the air, chances are you will lunge for each other's throat - something you don't want to happen. Once the fighting goes from verbal to physical, now you have a marriage that will soon become irreparable.

• Be clear

When it comes to resolving conflict, ensure that you are clear about what made you upset. For instance, instead of saying something like, "I hate how you show me disrespect," you may say, "I was upset that you spread rumors about me that I gave you an STD – herpes!" It becomes easier to resolve the issue when it has been stated clearly.

• Don't hit below the belt

Of course, during fights, it's hard to control what jumps out of our mouths. But still, you have to be careful that you don't go beyond the pale. It might cause your partner to resent you tremendously, causing irreconcilable differences. Some of the insults that hurt deeply are those touching on what the person has no control over, for instance, body appearance and health. Hitting below the belt can have the effect of making your partner hate both you and them for being in such a spot in the first place.

• Don't talk over each other

Resolving an issue can be particularly hard, especially when both sides feel they are right. This usually leads to both parties talking at once, and nothing makes sense. It amounts to wastage of time. Learn to take turns speaking so that everyone has a chance to express themselves.

• Don't be quiet

Not everyone reacts to conflict playfully; some clam up. But don't mistake their silence for a lack of emotions. Usually, such types have explosive emotions, but they do an excellent job of repressing them, which is not cool. As one bottles up their feelings, they slowly but steadily work their way toward a significant breakdown, where massive damage is guaranteed.

• Seek clarification

In the heated exchange of words, there can be many doubts. But don't let that happen. When you are in doubt, seek clarification. For instance, if your partner accuses you of cheating with someone named Jennifer, you might say, "I had group sex with Jennifer and her friends when you were out of the country – is that what you just said?" Restating what your partner says when in doubt will help you understand them clearly.

• Learn something

The fights that most couples get involved in stem from the fact that they haven't yet understood each other. As time passes and they learn what they care about, they will fight less and less. So, with every fight, ensure that you know something about yourself or your partner.

• Seek and implement changes

Now that you have fought over an issue, what's left is to ensure there's no repeat of the same. It is upon you to speak up about the changes you'd appreciate. It might be that you want your spouse to respect you more or to change their behaviors, but you have to state it and find out whether your partner is ready to comply. Just as important is your commitment to change in accordance with the wishes of your partner.

• Have a sense of humor

Fights bring out the drama queens and drama kings buried inside us. We go at our partners, aiming to inflict harm, and in the process, we create drama. Fights are nasty, but they may have some comedic value. Laugh at the silly things you said or did and then move on.

Chapter 5:
Misunderstandings—How to Prevent or Resolve Them

Misunderstandings are often one of the main reasons that relationships face disruption. It could be any relationship—one with your partner with your friends, colleagues, or even your family. But if you make an effort, you can generally avoid such misunderstandings or at least resolve them amicably. When your relationship is free of misunderstandings, you will experience peace of mind and be much happier with your partner.

Misunderstandings are quite common, and nearly everyone is disturbed by one at some point or the other. A misunderstanding can make you feel confused and distraught. It can affect your balanced state of mind and affect your relationship with the person involved. If this person is your partner, the misunderstanding can be especially harmful. No matter how stable and sturdy your relationship, a misunderstanding can throw it off balance. So many unfortunate people have broken off relationships with their significant others based on a single misunderstanding. Do you now get an idea of just how significant misunderstandings can be and why you need to avoid them?

So what is a misunderstanding? If you look at the word itself, you will see that it is the failure to understand or comprehend something properly. A misunderstanding has nothing right in it. It means you have failed to correctly understand a situation, a person, or the meaning behind their actions. A quarrel or disagreement is also a misunderstanding at times. It is a misinterpretation or distortion of reality. This is why misunderstandings leave the wrong impression. When you understand someone's words or actions in the wrong way, it is a misunderstanding. They might have done the same as well. The drawback is that it can be a real cause for trouble in your relationship and is probably one of the main reasons you both end up quarreling or upset with each other.

A misunderstanding does not always arise directly from how you communicate with a person. A lack of communication can even cause it. What you say, how you act, how you move, or even all that you don't do can give rise to misunderstandings in your relationship. For instance, when you don't call your partner for an entire day, they might misunderstand and assume you do not care about them. The real reason might be that you lost your phone, fell sick, or were too busy. These petty misunderstandings can cause unnecessary trouble in paradise. But in general, a misunderstanding is usually miscommunication and not the same as a lack of communication. Misunderstandings can be one-sided or even on the part of both partners. You might both misunderstand the other and interpret a situation, which, in reality, does not warrant any ill feelings.

What Causes Misunderstandings?

Various reasons can cause misunderstandings between you and your partner. Below are some of the common causes:

1. Words are interpreted in the wrong way and different from what the other person was trying to convey.

2. Something is not conveyed or explained in the right way, and the other person fails to understand.

3. You have prejudice and set notions in your mind that prevent you from making an unbiased interpretation.

4. Past behavior or instances are used as a reference, and your opinion is made based on them instead of the present.

5. A third person influences your thoughts and opinions. They can make you see things from their perception, and you may fail to see things with clarity.

6. You incorrectly assess a situation or a person.

7. You fail to understand the context of the matter.

8. You already mistrust the other person.

9. There are feelings of envy or jealousy.

10. There is a lack of self-esteem or self-confidence.

11. You get carried away by emotions.

There are plenty of other reasons that can make you or your partner misunderstand each other. In such cases, the assumptions you make will rarely have a justifiable reason and will be a projection of your emotions or thoughts.

Misunderstandings can happen in so many different ways. These days, there are more misunderstandings because of the prominent virtual world. There is so much miscommunication and misinterpretation of reality because of texts, images, etc. What you see will often make you assume things instantly. When you read something, you might be thinking of a different tone than what the person intended. Presumptions are usually made by the person who views or receives these kinds of messages and texts when the sender is unable to express them clearly. Such presumptions lead to misunderstandings.

How to Prevent Misunderstandings?

Communication is significant since it is only through conversations and opening up to each other that two individuals can truly expand their bond. However, regularly, we find that the end of a generally strong and cheerful relationship is miscommunication and misconception. Something can be seen in a very surprisingly different way from how it was intended. This usually prompts pointless fights that annihilate any feelings of closeness and fondness in the relationship.

This is why you should make it a point to practice mindful communication with your partner on a regular basis. Both of you should make an effort to have meaningful conversations that will help you to be transparent with each other. You should always make it a point to share whatever is at the forefront of your thoughts or in your heart. In the meantime, give your partner the room and opportunity to communicate well with you too. Try your best to always listen to your partner. You need to focus and truly listen to what they're trying to let you know. Keep in mind that communication is not just about saying whatever it is you need to say. It's about the steady trade of thoughts and emotions between two partners in a relationship. It's tied up with taking note of your partner's thoughts and feelings and attempting to see things from their point of view.

In the end, we are all just human, always prone to mistakes from time to time. That is all right. It's ordinary. Yet, in those instances of shortcoming, we need to try our best and take the appropriate actions to rectify our mistakes.

If you and your partner have been battling with misunderstandings in your relationship, you may find it confusing and troubling concerning how to approach settling them. Maybe you accidentally hurt your partner because of a misconception, or your partner hurt you, and you're trying to manage it. By figuring out how to speak with the one you cherish and become more attuned to the importance behind each other's words, you can attain a more satisfying relationship.

Paying attention and listening to your partner is vital to clearing up any misconceptions controlling your relationship in a negative way. Rather than simply waiting for one person to quit talking to say your bit, make it a point to concentrate on what he or she is saying. Listening is an important ability in creating and keeping a healthy relationship. You ought to listen as opposed to concentrating on how you need to react to or argue with what your partner is saying.

Establish common expectations in your relationship to clear up and stay away from problems later on. For instance, you may agree on the atmosphere you appreciate at home or the limitations of past relationships. Realizing how to best approach your partner when it comes to sensitive issues is useful to counteract misconceptions. You will learn that most couples don't have the habit of verbalizing what they need and want, which is a drawback.

While emails and messages are common methods of communication, they can prompt misunderstandings. It's difficult to sympathize with your partner when you can't even see their face or look into their eyes. On the off chance that your partner misjudges what you had truly implied in an email or instant message, make sure to account for yourself and clarify that you didn't finish the message you were trying to convey since it was only a short text. If these types of issues come up regularly, you both should decide to stop using electronic media. In case this isn't a choice, make a point to keep your electronic communications brief so as not to raise any significant life issues. You should not be fighting or breaking up over texts or social media.

If it so happens that your partner does something that confuses you or says something hurtful, don't make a hasty judgment about what their conduct or words mean. Maybe they were attempting to state something different but failed to convey it appropriately. Be purposeful about assuming the best about your partner. Rather than respond with resentment, take a few steps back and ask what they had implied by that specific statement. You will clear up misconceptions in your relationship by not making a hasty judgment, just as you figure out how to see each other in a more positive light.

Chapter 6:
How to Communicate About Serious Issues in Relationships

Why do you interact with your husband? Look no further; even if you don't know where to start, the steps below will help you connect with your spouse. It will also help you boost communication when things aren't going well in your marriage. And it all begins with you putting the seven basic steps shared below into practice. I have made use of these basic measures to strengthen communication in my marriage with great success. Personally, we agree that these communication techniques will allow you to start interacting with your spouse better today.

And if your partner doesn't want to practice them with you, you should practice them every day nonetheless, and it will strengthen your marriage.

Be Polite

Don't scream at your spouse when trying to get a message across or talk to each other. It just doesn't set the tone for effective communication. Why yell at your spouse? Ironically, we shout to be heard, but just causes our partner to scream back or shut down entirely. Speak in a calm and polite way. If you feel too upset or frustrated to do this, take a break and revisit the issue when both of you are calm. Be polite in your speech and be caring. It staves off conflict.

Walk a Mile in Your Wife's Shoes

If you have a debate, disagreement, try to look at the topic from the point of view of your partner. Seek to understand where the partner is coming from and continue listening empathetically. It will help you to understand what your partner is trying to say. How does your partner understand best you're trying to tell them? Are there certain words you need to say? Be mindful that they do think differently from you. Implement what you find out.

Strengthen Awareness

Just explain what you mean! Ask your partner if they understand what you're trying to get across. When they understand you completely, let them explain it back to you. What words do they use? This will indicate that they get what you are trying to communicate.

Changing Your Game and Hitting Home Run

When you partner doesn't understand what you have written, try to convey it using different methods. Seek various verbal examples, analogies, or even pictures, depending on what you are trying to convey.

Take a Rest

If you don't make progress in expressing a thought, concept, question and start getting irritated, take a break. Assess the effectiveness after each of you has had time to think about the problem. It's necessary and very helpful. Perhaps it's just time to re-evaluate. The pair's willingness to step back is necessary to enhance communication in every marriage. And you need to recognize that you and your partner must make a deliberate effort to connect effectively in your marriage. Additionally, by knowing how to better communicate with your spouse, you can avoid most of the communication issues and small (even some big) arguments in your marriage.

Marriage is Impossible Without Trust

Trust is a critical part of communication. A stable marriage can't exist without mutual confidence. Communication with each other, without confidence, will not be successful. The problems of confidence in marriage can be induced by physical affairs, deception, emotional affairs, contact with an ex, pornography, etc. A lack of confidence creates uncertainty in general. Building full trust in your marriage should always be a priority because it contributes to a deeper level of contact. Being able to trust your husband or wife gives you the confidence and freedom to express yourself entirely. Trust makes feel comfortable enough to share with your partner any part of yourself without fear of rejection or guilt. Likewise, your partner needs to be able to trust that the deep intimate issues you are thinking about and communicating with each other stay between you two.

Tips for Cultivating Trust in Your Marriage

- Promise each other and yourself that you will be frank and truthful even though it hurts.
- Share your experiences, in particular the stresses and hardships you face every day. Be emotionally aware.
- Avoiding lying or cheating by omission.
- Be mindful of the harm incurred, recognize and be liable for your wrongdoings.
- Stick with your words.
- Listen to your partner and pay heed.
- Give your partner the chance to gain trust.

- There is mutual faith in marriage; it takes two to bring that about.
- Be honest and be yourself.
- Be open to advise or see a marriage coach if appropriate.
- It needs time and patience — a lot of patience.
- Prove your love and respect for your partner.
- Set your marital limits to avoid a repetition of the same problems that created a breach of confidence.

Love and Respect

Respect is generally won, but often, without being warranted, it needs give and take. If you respond politely to your partner even though they may not be deserving of it, you'll have accomplished an act of selflessness.

You have to handle him/her with the respect that you yourself want to have. Respect the way you treat yourself. Respect the way money is spent. Honor your partner when with others or while you are alone. Show affection to your husband or wife in the way you speak or respond.

Love, love. It seems like our lives revolve around it. Our relationship with love is what allows us to believe we have a place on earth. Love can hurt sometimes, but we want to help you learn how to connect in love without harm. Communicating in love starts by knowing what you say or do before you do it, wanting the best for your partner, always holding it at the forefront of your mind. You're not without blame, and your partner is neither, so show them the same grace you would like. If you're not used to worrying a lot about your partner, it won't be easy, but you can do it.

Exercising Patience with Your Partner

Patience is another important factor for a good, happy, and safe marriage. Patience lets us connect quickly without getting upset. It is the ability to accommodate and prevent us from angry or irritating reactions.

Have you ever had a sluggish computer? What did you do while waiting? You either waited patiently or started moaning that this machine is sluggish. Maybe clicking vigorously or slammed the lid down. Would the machine work any quicker in either situation? The simple answer is no, but either waiting quietly or moaning has two different implications.

If your attitude is calm and optimistic, you become patient. Yet, when you complain and are pressed, your mood became hostile. On the basis of this example alone, we can understand that being optimistic can give us a more positive mood and outcome with our partners.

What does patience in marriage mean? How will it help you connect with your partner better? It means you have to be careful with your partner when, inadvertently, they hurt you or make you upset, and when your marriage is not what you want it to be.

Imagine scolding or yelling at your partner simply because you are upset about something insignificant. Now imagine you're in their shoes, and you're the one they're yelling at or belittling. Not a good feeling, right? The golden rule applies here, so make up your mind to treat your spouse the same way you want treatment. Respect your partner and love him or her!

There are also times when you can introduce flexibility while interacting with your partner. This is a regular need. Here are a few examples If you have a spousal dispute:

- If it appears your partner is not paying attention to you.
- If the partner needs to wait for the game to end to take the garbage out.
- Getting you late because your partner takes a long time to get ready to leave.

How angry do become in these examples? Being cooperative with your partner helps you to think before responding. Taking a pause will help you become more aware of your tone and whether you appear upset. That extra moment avoids a defensive reaction. Every day, you will find several instances where you can practice being cautious - with your spouse particularly.

When it comes to disagreeing with your partner, you must have patience. Even when you cool down, you have to pause and return to the discussion later, with time to reflect, and the same goes for your partner. It can be difficult to have patience if you want to fix issues quickly and not leave things hanging. Before you go to bed, you may have fixed everything, but occasionally, you might have to wait until the next morning to fix everything or ask someone for help.

You need caution when it comes to scheduling discussions that you know might be more active. Waiting for a deeper discussion, or one that might require some emotional pressure is best when both of you are comfortable and have a moment to yourselves.

To recap, patience with your spouse lets you think before you respond. Showing empathy to each other helps you interact without difficulty, argue less, and have peaceful discussions. This definitely favors successful marital communication.

Chapter 7:
The Role and Importance of Empathy in Your Relationship

People tend to confuse empathy with sympathy. However, you need to know the difference between the two. To have compassion for someone means to feel pity or sorrow for them when they face misfortune. To have empathy means being able to understand and share their feelings.

It is typical for people to disagree with each other on most things. Everyone has their own opinions and feelings. However, it is important to respect the other person's feelings and not try to railroad over them with your own. It is especially so in a relationship. You have to cultivate a sense of compassion and endure the other person's views and emotions. Empathy will allow you to do this and develop a strong relationship with your partner.

Influence of Empathy in a Relationship

You need to have empathy for your partner, and they should do the same for you too. When you can empathize with another person, you will feel what they are feeling to some degree. For instance, you will understand their pain or feel happy when they are happy. If you can develop empathy within yourself, you will perceive your partner's emotions even as they keep changing. It is crucial to understand each other and provide support when needed. Having empathy will help you become more compassionate. Developing compassion in yourself is important as it makes you want to help your partner in their time of need and provide them with the care they require.

If you fail to have empathy for the other person, you will not have compassion either. You will fail to recognize their emotions and thus fail to react appropriately. According to many studies, people who lack empathy are usually the ones who are mean to others. They fail to understand how their words and actions affect the other person. Such people lie to themselves and refuse to take responsibility for their actions. They rarely show remorse for hurting another person. It can harm all their relationships in life regardless of whether it is at work or home.

Empathy is actually at the heart of a happy relationship. Your relationship will struggle to survive when it lacks empathy. You will lack compassion without empathy, and this will affect the bond you have with your partner. Empathy is like a bridge between two individuals who have different feelings, thoughts, or perspectives. Empathy can be of three types.

- Cognitive empathy is when you can look at things from another person's perspective but cannot feel their emotions. It allows you to appreciate the situation the other person is going through.

- Emotional empathy allows you to feel what the other person is feeling or thinking. It allows you to connect with the person more emotionally.

- Compassionate empathy is what you need to develop to a greater extent within yourself. Cognitive or emotional empathy can often have a negative impact. For instance, someone can use it to manipulate someone for their benefit. But with compassionate empathy, you will feel compassion and be less inclined to want to harm anyone. If you have compassionate empathy, you will think twice before you do anything and be more considerate of your partner's feelings. If you know that your partner feels annoyed or frustrated when the room is messy, you will empathize and keep it clean. Your empathy will help you become a good partner, and they will appreciate your efforts. Compassionate empathy will help you respond to your partner with love, compassion, and understanding.

How to Develop Empathy

Now that you recognize the importance of it, you should try to nurture empathy within yourself. The following steps will help you in becoming more empathetic.

<u>Increase your self-awareness</u>. When you become more attuned to your own emotions and thoughts, you will also recognize them in others. If something hurts you, you will know that it could hurt another person too. Take notice of how you feel and think when your partner is saying or doing something. Don't be too absorbed in yourself and learn to exert control over the way you react.

<u>Practice self-empathy</u>. You will fail to empathize with your partner when you cannot sympathize with yourself. You need to pay attention to your own emotions and acknowledge when you are going through a difficult time. Taking care of yourself should always be a priority. Don't compromise self-care in an attempt to take care of your partner. You can face your issues without catastrophic about it. Remaining calm and composed will help you meet everything that comes your way.

<u>Pay attention to body language</u>. Be careful about your body language

and learn to observe that of others as well. A person's gestures, expressions, and various movements can tell a lot about their feelings.

<u>Observe nonverbal cues</u>. How a person says something is often more revealing than what they are saying. The nonverbal cues will help to identify their emotional truth.

<u>Develop the habit of listening well</u>. You won't empathize with someone if you don't even listen to what they are saying. Pay attention to the details, and be a good listener. Avoid interrupting someone when they talk. Too many people are focused on talking more than listening. Give genuine attention to your partner at all times. Even when you argue, don't be focused on finding a way to defend yourself. Focus on what they are saying and try to understand their perspective.

<u>Look for the positive aspects of your partner and your relationship</u>. When you concentrate too much on the negative, you affect your ability to empathize healthily. Start taking note of the good things instead of constantly thinking of the bad.

<u>Avoid being judgmental or doubting what the other person says</u>. Listen with an open heart and mind. Don't focus too much on giving advice or telling them what they should or should not do. When a person shared their problem, they trust you and are looking for support. Be more focused on listening than trying to solve the problem. Keep your own opinions and values aside and focus on what the other person feels and needs from you. Being too entangled in your perspective will prevent you from acting mindfully toward your partner.

Use these tips to develop a sense of empathy for your partner and others. It will make a lot of difference in how you communicate with people, and it will positively improve your relationships with them.

How to Communicate with Empathy

Now that you understand a little more about empathy, you have to start communicating with it in mind. If you are experiencing finding the right things to say, the following statements might help you figure it out.

Acknowledge your partner's pain. You need to acknowledge how they feel at all times. They will feel supported when you connect with their struggle or pain. You may use the following sentences:

1. "I am sorry that you have to go through this."
2. "I hate that this happened to you."
3. "This must be hard for you."
4. "I can see that this must be a difficult situation for you."

Share your feelings. You can be truthful and admit it when you don't know what to say or do. It is not always easy to imagine what the other person is going through. Share your thoughts and let your partner know that you are trying. You may use the following sentences:

- "I wish I could make things better."
- "My heart hurts for you."
- "I'm really sad that this happened to you."
- "I'm sorry that you are feeling this way."

Show your partner that you are grateful when they open up to you. People find it difficult to open up and be vulnerable to others. More often than not, their trust has been broken at some point. So when they choose to trust you, you need to be grateful and express it. Show your partner you appreciate that they share their thoughts and emotions with you. Acknowledge how difficult it can be for them to do this sometimes. You may use the following sentences:

- "I'm glad that you shared this with me."
- "I'm glad that you are telling me this."
- "I can imagine how hard it must be to talk about this. Thank you for sharing it with me."
- "I appreciate you trying to work hard on our relationship. I know you are trying, and that gives me hope."

Show your partner that you are interested in. You have to take an interest in what your partner is going through. It can be hard to go through difficult times alone. You have to reach out and show them that you are there for support. Show them that you are listening to whatever they have to say. Don't offer too much advice or too many opinions. Just be a good listener. You may use the following sentences:

- "How are you feeling about all that's been going on lately?"
- "I think you're feeling like ——. Am I right? Did I misunderstand?"
- "What has this been like for you?"

Show encouragement. When your partner or spouse is going through a tough time, you have to be encouraging. But you need to go about this the right way. Don't try to fix their problem or offer unsolicited advice. Just encourage them in a way that makes them feel better and motivated. Show them that you care and that you believe in them. You may use the following sentences:

1.   "You are strong, and I believe you can get through this."

2.   "I am always on your side. You should never feel alone."

3.   "I'm proud of everything that you have done."

4.   "You matter, and you should never question it."

5.   "You are a very talented person."

Chapter 8:
How to Improve Communication Between Couples?

We're talking about day-to-day communication, the nitty-gritty, the getting-on-the-same page kind of stuff that can be tricky, especially if you and your partner are very different. Being different doesn't mean you can't communicate well, however. Here are some ideas on how to build up that area of your relationship:

Learn your partner's love language

When you communicate with your partner in a way they connect with, it shows you care. It shows you are paying attention. They will feel loved, safe, secure, and happy. These emotions are all essential to a healthy relationship between two people who trust each other.

You can figure out your partner's love language by looking at how they tend to express love to you and others. As an example, are they known for their unique and thoughtful gifts at birthdays and holidays? Or are they always willing to drop whatever they're doing to take a phone call from a friend or sit on the couch and listen when you need to talk? Maybe they are always touching you in some way, like giving you a backrub when you're watching TV together or holding your hand in the car. In order, those love languages were Giving/Receiving Gifts, Quality Time, and Physical Touch. Once you've identified your partner's love language, start showing them attention in the appropriate ways.

Engage in a small talk

Small talk is how a couple probably got to know each other in the first place, and it's what keeps a relationship interesting and fun. If you feel yourself drifting from your partner emotionally, some light conversation and joking around might be what you two need. Small talk can also help people who aren't natural sharers. Often, this type of person simply isn't used to talking about themselves, and fun conversational subjects can help get them used to it without the added pressure of emotional heaviness.

Examples of small talk questions:

"What's your all-time favorite movie or TV show so far this year?"

"Did anything funny happen to you today?"

"How's that book you're reading?"

"Who do you think is going to win the game tomorrow?"

"If you could go anywhere on vacation this year, where would you go?"

Share your experiences

One great way for a couple to get more in sync and emotionally on the same page is to share their experiences. The power of storytelling and narrative has been studied for centuries, and it's something that all people have in common. We all connect to a good story. By communicating to your partner through sharing stories about your past, what happened during your day, and more, you're inviting them into your shoes. You're encouraging empathy. It's also useful for you because you learn how to verbalize your feelings and reactions to things that have happened. Events, whether they're normal ones or traumatic ones, can become more tangible and manageable if shared with your partner.

Examples of experiences to share with a partner:

- Embarrassing moments as a child
- What it felt like when your grandparent/other loved one passed away
- What it felt like to start a new job
- What it felt like the first time you flew in an airplane
- What it felt like when you heard your favorite song for the first time
- Funny moments with your high school/college/work friends

Have regular check-ins

Part of good communication is being consistent. You don't want a day to go by without some kind of check-in. Based on your and your partner's schedules, choose a time of day to have a brief talk, even if it's just a rundown of what happened that day and how you're feeling.

For some people, right before bed is a great time when they've set aside the day's distractions and can focus on their partner. For others, that's not a good time because they're ready just to pass out. Over dinner, when you've both had some time to wind down from the day, might be better. If you're both early birds, a talk in the morning over breakfast or coffee could work. If you're apart and too busy to physically meet, have a phone call during a work break. The list of options for daily check-ins is long.

If a short daily talk isn't enough, schedule a weekly date night where you two go out and have a more thorough check-in. This might be the best route for parents since it can be hard to find a good time when they aren't distracted by the kids. Have a reliable babysitter, go to a cozy restaurant and be a couple. As we've said and will keep saying, every couple is different, and every individual is other. Figure out what works for you.

Communication exercises + games

The last handy way to improve your communication with your partner is to try out communication exercises and games. These are often employed in a couples therapy setting, but they're easy to do by yourself, too. You also don't need to be in therapy to get something out of them. Here are some excellent examples:

Twenty Questions

This classic game is entertaining and can trigger some great conversations. Come up with 20 questions (or look online) for your partner and take turns asking and answering them back and forth. They can be light-hearted like, "What's your favorite fruit?" or more serious, like "When have you felt the most scared?"

Look Into My Eyes

One of the more intimate games out there, "Look Into My Eyes," is all about vulnerability. Sit facing each other, close enough to hold hands. Look deeply into your partner's eyes for a few minutes, not speaking and not looking away. Take note of the feelings that arise in you. After a few minutes, start talking about something, like how your day was. Stay in eye contact. When you've finished talking, it's your partner's turn. Go back and forth a few times. Afterward, describe how this exercise made you feel.

Giving Thanks

Set aside some time with your partner. Both think about three good things that your partner did for you, whether it was helping you with the dishes, sending you a funny text, or giving you a back rub. Be sure to say, "Thank you." This exercise helps both people take note of the positive things in the relationship and express gratitude.

Highs and Lows

This game is a great one for daily check-ins. It's best played during the evening, but not too late when both or one of you is tired. Ask your partner what the high and low of their day was and then share your own. While your partner is talking, practice good listening techniques like eye contact, nodding, asking questions, and so on. This will build empathy and encourage your partner to be open and honest.

Simon Says/Copycat

First, one of you should draw something on a piece of paper. Think structures like boats, animals, and so on. Now, without showing your partner your drawing, walk them through how to copy it on their piece of paper. Don't tell them what it is; go line by line. Pretend as if they've never seen a cat or a boat, so those words don't mean anything. This game challenges your ability to communicate clearly in a way your partner understands, and it challenges their ability to listen.

Chapter 9:
Active Listening

Active listening is a conscious approach and one that aims to understand the speaker and aid their communication through an appropriate response.

What Does it Mean to Actively Listen?

Active listening is a communication skill that recognizes listening as an active role in conversation; it validates responses and keeps the conversation going by providing feedback and demonstrating understanding. Its aim is to understand the other person's communication and demonstrate this understanding.

There are many different motivations for listening, which can be seen in the types of listening mentioned above. Whatever the appropriate type, an active listener is motivated to understand the message, eliminating their bias and listening flaws, and actively seeking to engage with the speaker.

The term "active listening" originally referred to a communication technique used in counseling, which involved the listener giving feedback, and often paraphrasing or rephrasing what they hear to demonstrate their understanding, to confirm that their understanding is in line with the speaker's meaning.

Active listening is an extension of this concept, an application to a variety of settings. Dynamic-active listening is the term used when you take this valuable counseling technique and apply it to everyday communication settings, and relationships.

Passive – vs. – Active Listening

Study the chart below to understand the difference between passive listening, and active listening:

Active	Passive
Focused Attention: an active listener does not only hear the sounds and words. They focus their attention long enough to begin the process of listening.	Not focused or pretending to be paying attention: a passive listener is often not paying full attention, if they are paying any at all. In an attempt to appear as though they are listening, a passive listener may pretend to show that they are listening.
Want to understand speaker's message: an active listener genuinely wants to understand what is being communicated, and the level it is being communicated at. The speaker's message is what is most important to them.	Not aimed at understanding the speaker's message: a passive listener, because of a variety of reasons; be it lack attention, or severe bias, or a combative listening style, aims for something other than understanding the speaker's intended message. They are instead waiting for the speaker to stop talking, or for their opportunity to say their own point.

Adapts to context described here as dynamic listening, active listeners try to grasp the context of an interaction and adapt their listening to follow suite.	Is not concerned with context: a passive listener is not paying enough attention or is only concerned with themselves in the interaction. If you are listening passively, you may therefore miss the point entirely; neglecting the emotions of the speaker where that is the level they are trying to engage at, for example.
Tries to eliminate personal bias and judgment as well as adapting to the context and requirements of the speaker, the active listener must try to suspend their own bias and judgment and understand their own perceptual filter. By taking this approach, they can better understand the speaker's intended message.	Often filters out information through bias or judgement: a passive listener may have a bias towards the speaker, or towards the speaker's message. They may therefore often misinterpret the message, concerned only with their own opinions.

Provides feedback: active listening wants to understand the message, and also to encourage the speaker to feel understood, and to elaborate if they want to. An active listener therefore gives good feedback, in the form of paraphrasing, questions, and other responses	Does not provide feedback, or provides very little, or meaningless feedback because a passive listener is not actually listening to understand the message, they are unlikely to be able to properly encourage the speaker. They may give a nod or two, but they will not be able to give real feedback. Have you ever found yourself struggling to finish your point because the speaker has not given any indications that they are following? They were listening passively, or not at all.
Gives good non-verbal responses: part of the feedback that constantly occurs during conversation, is non-verbal. Because an active listener is fully engaged, they are likely to give good eye-contact, lean forward to show interest, make facial expressions to match the emotions they are feeling, and nod to show that they are understanding.	Lacks non-verbal engagement: in the same way that a passive listener provides less verbal feedback, they will also be noticeably less engaged in non-verbal communication. This is perhaps even more obvious than with verbal feedback, which is easier to fake. A passive listener therefore may display less eye contact, and their body language will not encourage the speaker.

Takes responsibility for playing an active role in conversation: an active listener sees listening in a positive light and takes responsibility for their role in the interaction. They therefore try to be well rounded and complete, understanding what is being communicated, giving feedback to demonstrate their understanding, and then responding smoothly to move between the role of listener and speaker.	Passive outlook on listening: a passive listener does not engage the speaker well, rarely understands the full extent of the message, and does not give enough feedback for either person to feel satisfied in the interaction. This is largely because a passive listener does not recognize the value or take responsibility for their role as a listener.

Why Active Listening is Important

There are many reasons why active listening is important, and many benefits it can bring to your life, especially where it concerns a relationships with loved ones.

- <u>Avoid Misunderstandings</u>- Misunderstandings often arise from miscommunications where the message of the speaker is lost in translation or is disregarded. Think about the last time you had an argument or misunderstanding with your spouse? Probably the last time one or both of you did not listen to the other. Active listening can help you to avoid such misunderstandings.

- <u>Find Resolutions to Problems and Disagreements</u>- Nothing can ever be resolved in you are not prepared to listen.

Whenever a problem or disagreement arises it is often best solved through active listening, understanding your loved ones, and their perspective on the situation, as well as expressing your own.

- <u>Useful for Work and Business</u>- active listening can equally be applied to a work or business environment, where understanding and listening to colleagues, partners, and yes, even your boss, is likely to help to improve life, and help you to secure deals.

- <u>Learn more effectively</u>- When a friend has something to teach, then you have something to learn! With active listening, and an understanding of the type of listening that will most benefit you (usually informative for learning skills), you will find that you can enjoy a dynamic that encourages not only learning, but a solid respect and therefore an improved relationship.

- <u>Understand Your Loved Ones</u>- Active listening is not only about damage control and avoiding conflict. It brings about a great understanding of the people around you. Through active listening, you begin to see interactions as a way of understanding a person, their perspective, their emotions, and their point of view. Passive listening does none of this; it is closed off from understanding the real message of the interaction. Active listening always aims for more understanding.

- <u>Improve Relationships</u>- All this leads to an improvement in your relationships. A greater understanding, a greater ability to avoid conflict, and to overcome problems, a greater ability to learn and to appreciate the perspectives of other people; all of this leads to a vast improvement in personal relationships.

6 Steps to Active Listening

- <u>Pay Attention</u>- There is not much chance of listening without it, and it is something that by now you should know the importance of. Without attention you will not even hear the message of the speaker, let alone listen to it. If you are sitting in a room full of loud noises and electronic distractions then this will be difficult, so eliminate as many distractions as possible if you want to have successful interactions. Aside from this, the main idea is to be interested in what is being said; you must want to listen and therefore your attention will naturally be on the message of the speaker.

- <u>Understand the Context</u>- It is the process of understanding the context of the conversation and adapting to the needs of the speaker. If your friend is teaching you to fish, then you should be listening for the information you need to learn how to do it. If your child is telling you about their day at school, you should be listening to their feelings, thinking about whether they are happy.

- <u>Show That You Are Listening</u>- As an active listener, you should be giving off a good amount of verbal and non-verbal cues, to let the speaker know that you are engaged in what they are saying. Nothing is more off-putting for your spouse than receiving no signals that you are listening; they are speaking, and you are staring blankly at the TV with your hands down your pants! Instead, you should engage with eye-contact, lean forward to show attention and interest, nod and give facial expressions, and give small verbal cues, such as saying "yes". This is part of the feedback process.

- <u>Defer Judgment</u>- It is important that you defer judgment until after the speaker has finished their message. In this way you are able to focus on understanding your loved ones, which is the whole aim of active listening. Try to eliminate your perceptual bias, or at least be aware of it. As thoughts, feelings, and opinions arise, let them wash over you and focus your attention on the speaker's message, not on your own potential responses.

- <u>Give Feedback</u>- Feedback is related to showing that you are listening but takes it further; good feedback shows that you are understanding what is being said. You are relaying your understanding back to the speaker to check that you have properly understood to allow them chance to correct your understanding, and so that you both feel satisfied that you are "on the same page" so to speak. In giving good feedback, you are making sure the speaker feels understood, and valuable.

- <u>Responding Appropriately</u>- You may be wondering about how far to take your role as an active listener? Conversation and interaction are, after all, a dynamic process between speaker and listener. If you only ever listened you would not have an input in the conversation, and that is not the idea of active listening.

Active listening is about understanding the listener's message so that you can improve your relationships and your understanding of your loved ones. You may want to give your own opinions, show support, digress into another conversation or example from your own life, elaborate, or take the conversation in a totally different direction.

Chapter 10:
Communication on Financial Management

When a man and a woman are living as a couple, or when they have a wedding project ahead, it is rare to hear them discuss the topic of financial management. However, according to several studies, the monetary question is at the origin of many divorces. Being in a relationship is not just about love. It's nice to love each other, but it does not pay for shopping, cinema or traveling to Beijing. So how do you manage your money in a relationship? Of course, as there is no one way to be in love, there is no miracle recipe for managing one's finances with one's life partner. That may be why we sometimes see marvelous relationships that end in violent conflict because of money. Thus, to avoid those money management problems which are a real wasp nest for your marriage, here are some tips.

Set Priorities

In the life of a couple, it is perfectly reasonable and understandable that everyone has different habits and desires. And it is normal to try to answer them reasonably, without penalizing one or the other. Only, it must be noted that life as a couple requires a certain number of choices, even sacrifices. It's therefore imperative to know how to make choices while taking into consideration the desires of one another.

Also, it is vital to define the way of working together, to establish a budget, even prematurely, and to think about savings and investments. It is normal for couples to divide their daily tasks to make their lives easier. However, when it comes to your financial strategy, it's important to talk about it and choose a line to follow. You probably have joint projects that require individual and collective sacrifices, upon which you will have to agree. Listening is the best way to getting along.

The three healthy ways of spending in a relationship: the financial management of the couple is a spectrum built around three methods: equity, half and a half and pooling. There is a brilliant idea when both of you agree. Fairness means that everyone participates according to their income. Sometimes one spouse earns significantly more than the other or has special needs. They can, therefore, contribute more without it being unfair. Half and a half are the methods that will prevail when both members of the couple have the same financial personality (debt, leisure, income). They will share the expenses. Pooling is acting without regard to who pays what. The couple serves as a single entity in revenues and expenditures.

Communicating with Your Spouse

Even if one decides to have separate accounts and finances, it is essential to talk with one's spouse about everything related to investments (loans and outstanding debts). You should never have financial secrets. Having secret accounts could be the source of unpleasant surprises if one of the two partners disappeared or is deceased. It is an obnoxious assumption but still possible, so being aware of the reports and accounts of the deceased simplifies the life of the survivor.

Create a Common Account

Couples will have to choose how they will manage their money in a financial institution. This comes down to three choices, too: joint account, a separate account or both.

Separate accounts allow clearly seeing the expenses and contribution of each. Each spouse can, therefore, bear his share of responsibility, and the balance is quickly found. However, this solution may sometimes not be optimal. A couple is also a two-person adventure that involves a lot of shared expenses. Tracking can become complicated. The joint account makes it easier to keep track of the couple's expenses. For those who wish to pool their money, this can be a good solution. That said, the joint account requires more control and consultation to avoid unpleasant surprises. But, while maintaining a certain autonomy and a personal financial space, it is possible to spend together on joint projects. This is the best of both systems but also concentrates on their faults. It will require more logistics.

The creation of a standard account makes it possible to simplify the participation of each one in the ordinary expenses and the follow-up of the costs and the budget. Then you have to feed the account for the ordinary expenses. Each spouse has, of course, the freedom to keep a personal account, which he can manage independently by keeping a discretionary income.

As for the management of this account, we must try to allocate the funds to the common priorities. We must also try to be rigorous, but without depriving ourselves of everything. This would mean that if one spouse needs something that does not jeopardize the couple's finances, the other spouse should allow him or her to buy it.

Once you have made the financial decisions, you can go about your relationship without worrying more than you need to about money. In the end, good accounts make good relationships.

Balancing the Budget

Achieve and maintain a balanced budget by dividing ordinary expenses based on each person's income. As an illustration, if one of the two spouses earns 10,000 euros while the other earns 5,000 euros, the one who makes more should assume two-thirds of the domestic expenses, while the other one would pay just the remaining third.

As soon as the situation of the couple evolves, it is necessary to adjust and adapt the budget. Take the case of a growing family buying a house. Plus, not living beyond one's means is an excellent way to reach a balanced budget to build precautionary savings and reserve an investment pool of money.

We must at all costs limit purchases on credit and, above all, question our consumption habits. Small daily and recurring expenses that are not essential can be nice sums for a better use.

If one of the spouses is thrifty while the other is a spender, try to find a balance by defining the tasks of each person. In other words, it is imperative to establish who does what. The ideal would be a good manager who deals with the management of high finances. But communication must remain and decision-making shared.

Even if you do not have investments, a financial advisor can be of great help. You can start with your banker, for example. To be satisfied with only with your banker is, however, not judicious. An experienced investment adviser is always judicious. Of course, you could be autonomous and keep control of your investments.

Contrary to what you might imagine, it is not that complicated. Many sites and blogs provide good advice. If you are not trained and wholly independent, advice from a financial advisor is warranted. Ask relevant questions and be sure of your choices.

Money can be a source of trouble and discord in your marriage. Take the lead, and these tips should help you.

One last tip: do not hesitate to address the subject out of fear. The question of money will come sooner or later. So, go for it! By explaining your approach, any lingering doubts will be lifted. And then you will pass for someone responsible and proactive.

Chapter 11:
Common Relationship Conflicts

All relationships will have conflicts—there is no doubt about it. If you think you have the unicorn relationship where you and your partner never communicate harshly or out of frustration, or that you will never ever have a conflict, then think again. We all have conflicts with our partners at times. Just by being with each other constantly, you are quite likely to run into problems.

You will get to know each of the usual issues closely to see the interactions between you and your partner in a new light. Make sure you take the time to work with your problems. They are problems that you can actively begin to eliminate from your relationship. However, to eliminate these problems, you have to try. You cannot simply duck your head between your knees and assume they will go away.

Selfishness

Selfishness is often the underlying factor of many different conflicts, whether we realize it or not. Think about it—if your long-term partner made a major decision that significantly impacts you without any input from you, how would you feel? Most people would be entirely furious. They would feel like their partner was fundamentally selfish. If you cannot trust your partner to let you weigh in on those big decisions, you probably will feel pretty bad. You may feel like your partner does not care about you or is simply unwilling to see that you disagree. You would call them selfish.

It is difficult in relationships to tow that line between being too controlling and having your say. You are encouraged to be your person. Still, in long-term relationships, especially marriage or when two people commit to being life partners, it is hard to see that you can truly begin interacting in a way that is not smothering. Where do you draw the line? What needs to be communicated? What does not? Where do you think that you can make decisions on your own?

In reality, you are always free to make your own decisions so long as you realize the aftermath, too. If you want to make those selfish decisions, you must also respect the fact that it could mean the end of your relationship.

Think about it—if you want a child, but your partner went out and got permanent birth control without letting you know that they were considering it, would you think of them as selfish? If a child is the last thing you want in life, but your partner does, who is the selfish one there? Who wins?

Ultimately, when that selfishness is allowed to win, it ends in failure. It shows a fundamental incompatibility in the relationship, which sometimes happens without you being able to manage or control it. That is just the way of life; if you can accept it, you are more likely to succeed. You need to figure out how to communicate and solve those conflicts that come from selfishness.

A Lack of Communication

A lack of communication creates problems in all areas of a relationship. Without communication, there is no relationship at all. Still, too much communication and talking without thinking can also breed conflict, so where do you find that middle ground? When do you say, this is how you are going to do things? That line in the sand is highly important, and without it, you will struggle.

You need to learn how to communicate and how to talk openly in any relationship. Lacking this is a recipe for disaster. Let's go right back to that example about selfishness: it is selfish not to communicate about getting on a permanent form of birth control, for example, if you know that your partner wants and is trying for children. You know that your lack of communication about the matter will lead to your partner not getting what he or she wants, allowing them to continue trying and not knowing it is not possible. While you are within your right to get birth control, if you choose to do so, it is still wrong not to communicate with your partner if it is going to limit or prevent them from achieving their dream. You need to figure out how to communicate enough and work together as a team but not enough to cause conflict in the first place - and that is tough.

Resentment

Resentment is the silent killer of all relationships, and of all of the possibilities that have been mentioned thus far, this is the most fatal when it comes to relationships. You must understand that resentment is not okay—it stews and impacts relationships heavily. Before you know it, you find that nothing matters at that point, and the resentment is too much.

At some point in time, you will offend your partner. It is only natural in any relationship. However, if your partner never tells you they are upset and simply stews in their anger, there will be a major problem. Your partner will begin to hold onto that negativity until it turns into resentment. There will be no healing, no fixing what has gone wrong. Rather, you will find that the relationship itself will suffer and quite possibly fail.

Resentment will, over time, lead to the relationship completely degrading. The individual's discontent will eventually become so strong that they will believe they do not want to be in the relationship anymore. They will distance themselves as they cannot cope with the negativity. As a direct result, you end up with a relationship that is suffering or even dying.

You cannot hold onto negativity, and mindfulness is the perfect way to fix the problem. When you can think and act mindfully, you avoid the problem. You can make sure that you act in ways that will allow for solving conflicts when they arise instead of allowing them to fester endlessly until the relationship fails.

Criticism

Another common problem in relationships is criticism When you criticize everything your partner does, you will most likely frustrate them beyond anything else. Think about it—how would you like it if everything you did was wrong and everything that goes wrong is your fault. Sometimes, one person is in the wrong or one person's overarching habits are the issue in the first place, and they genuinely need fixing. However, approaching the situation harshly or unkindly is also a problem. You must approach relationships with kindness and respect. Mind the fact that you are talking to another person—one who you claim to love—and if you are treating them negatively, constantly, they are going to become a problem very quickly.

Criticism has no place in any relationship. You should not be saying negative things without offering up something constructive. It is okay to point out if they have messed up - if you do so kindly - while also suggesting what needs to be fixed. This is dramatically different than telling them that they are a total failure. You must remember that you need to avoid criticism unless you want to put up with all the fights that will come after.

Unfair or Unrealistic Expectations

Finally, one last point to consider as a major cause of conflict in relationships is unrealistic expectations. Think of all of the fairy tales and Disney movies you probably grew up watching. What was the general rule? It typically played out as the guy always gets the girl, and they always find the perfect partner. Prince Charming always comes around to save the day, and they live happily ever after, right?

Well, real life is not like that. While you may have believed that the perfect person for you is out there somewhere, that is not the case. There is no such thing as perfect. The only relationships that come across as perfect are the result of countless hours of effort. You cannot simply have the best, most positive relationship because it simply is not there. You cannot go into a relationship with unrealistic expectations without setting you and your partner up for failure.

The perfect partner does not exist, but you and your partner can cultivate a relationship that is right for both of you. You can learn to be respectful, caring, compassionate, and empathetic. You can be there for each other even when no one else is. You can partner with each other to the best of your ability. You can learn to love each other and be each other's unyielding sense of support. However, you will not simply find the perfect prince or princess that sweeps you off your feet and fall heads over heels in love with you. Let go of that notion right now or kiss your relationship goodbye.

Chapter 12:
Communicating Through Conflict in Marriage

When faced with a conflict in your marriage, think about how you express your feelings or talk about the conflict with your spouse. Good communication is where everyone can take stock and try to understand the attitude of the other. The conflict will be easier to manage when angry tones and unnecessary insults do not exacerbate it. For effective conflict communication, there are three rules to follow:

- Avoid raising your voice and keep calm whenever a conflict happens.
- Allow your spouse to talk and develop their argument because communication not only involves talking but also listening.
- Find a middle ground, but do not make compromises that can have negative consequences in the future.
- A couple who argues but who respects these three rules will find it easier to resolve a resolution.

Marriage is not always easy, and you are constantly learning. Is it possible not to repeat the same mistakes and stabilize one's romantic relationship? How can you manage conflicts in your relationships without becoming a doormat?

Follow these recommendations to rebuild the love in a struggling marriage:

- Once you understand the reasons for the tensions that are shaking your marriage, you can move on to the more "direct" phase of reconciliation. The first step can be very psychological because you have to communicate with your spouse.

- It is necessary to put in place more technical and thoughtful actions to find your spouse's heart and overcome the crisis of your marriage.

- The actions you have decided to put in place must correspond to the different issues; otherwise, the latter will not have any particular effects and aggravate the situation. Don't seek resolution just to be done with it - seek resolution to make it better.

- Don't assign blame on either side. Marriage is a team effort, and both of you need to be in it fully, or not at all.

- If your spouse or you are not feeling fulfilled in your marriage, you need to spend time together to understand better your issues and what you need from the relationship.

- Every marriage experiences conflict at one point or the other. It is important to know that disagreement is not necessarily a bad thing. It is a way in which people express their diverse views on a situation or topic.

Conflict Resolution in Healthy Relationships

Communication is the fuel that sustains a relationship. When we say a relationship is healthy, it means the partners value communication, and they never allow a lack of communication to affect their togetherness.

It is normal to disagree on some matters; however, constant conflict is a sign of an unhealthy relationship. Therefore, if you argue with your partner on trivial issues like the kinds of friends you hang out with, where to go for dinner or date night, and who should take care of which household chores, these tips are for you. They will help you resolve all your arguments amicably.

Do Not Cross Your Boundaries

Treat everyone with the respect they deserve, whether you are angry. Don't respond kindly if your partner ridicules you, calls you names and uses provocative words during an argument. Rather than replying to them, stay calm and walk away if they do not yield to your plea to stop. Let them know that you can proceed with the argument when tensions are lower.

Find the Root of the Matter

The argument does not just happen; there must be a reason for it. So, an effective way to get a conflict solved is by unmasking the real issue. Try to understand your partner. Maybe they might need special attention or are just feeling insecure. Knowing the primary cause of an argument will help you to get it solved amicably. The summary of the point we're trying to make here is that you should not shy away from the real issue.

Always Resolve Conflicts

Never pretend that all is well while you have something building inside you. Your goal is to have a healthy relationship, so everything needs to be out in the open. Indeed, you cannot always be on the same page, but you must respect each other's differences.

Compromise When Necessary

Compromise is one of the ingredients of a healthy relationship. You don't have to be dead set on winning the argument every time. There are some situations you have to let go of and accept that you are wrong.

Take Note of Everything

You must not be indifferent to your partner. You should consider the things that upset them and consider if you are taking advantage of them or being considerate enough. From which angle does your partner view issues? You need to find answers to these and many more questions to help you better understand your partner.

If you have tried all the tricks and the arguments persist, you should now look into the area of compatibility. Are you compatible with each other? If the answer is yes, learn to work with each other and implement all you have learned from this guide.

Conflict is a way of expressing your differences, but it should not degenerate into physical attacks or raining abuses on each other. It is never acceptable and is, in fact, the opposite of a healthy relationship. Never allow verbal abuse on either side and know when to end an argument if you discover that it is going in that direction.

Remember the knowledge that one of the signs of an unhealthy relationship is when a partner has a domineering attitude and tries to manipulate or control the other at all times.

On a final note, pay attention to what upsets your partner. Here are some of the things that may annoy your partner:

1.   You are always making excuses not to do things with them (and maybe ask yourself why you do this).

2.   Rather than spending time with your partner, you went out with friends (do you spend an equal amount of time with your partner and friends?)

3.   Not giving them your attention when they speak.

4.   You don't reply to their text or call after a reasonable amount of time.

Chapter 13:
Loving Words Heal Relationships

The two most dominant phrases that heal a harmed relationship are the hardest to state, "I'm sorry" and "I was wrong." It is basic in healing relationships for couples.

The motivation behind why these phrases are the hardest to state is because we would prefer not to admit that we have caused whatever has broken or harmed a relationship. More often than not, we say that it was the other person's deficiency. Also, we hang tight for that person to be the first to apologize. In any case, the apology never comes because the other person is likewise hanging tight for it.

What's more, we realize that relationships inside the family and outside of it sometimes end in the absence of this apology. We know many separations happen just because neither partner makes a move to apologize.

Why is it so challenging to admit that we weren't right and to apologize? It is straightforward that it is a human instinct, a shortcoming that puts us over the others. What we need is to defeat this commitment to self. It requires personal development, compassion, and thinking about the other. What's more, a necessary apology will reestablish that broken relationship.

It doesn't make a difference who fouled up when a relationship is broken. Significantly, we venture out. Remember that the other person feels a similar way. We should state something that can prompt healing, for example, "I'm sorry that we are having this issue.

Would we be able to discuss making things right once more?"

Making a stride like this quite often prompts healing a broken relationship. Furthermore, more often than not, the conversation results in the two gatherings saying "sorry", which typically leads to a more grounded relationship.

Any healing in a relationship for couples requires some forgiveness. It should originate from the heart before it is said in words.

One must be cautious about that as it may in communicating forgiveness. To state, "I forgive you", amidst a battle may be misjudged as, "You weren't right", and would compound the situation. We should say, "I forgive you", just when the other person requests forgiveness. At that point, these become the ideal words. Mercy can heal the relationship as well as the bodies and the brains of the two persons. Keep in mind that in healing relationships for couples, we as of now have the words. We need to state them. Have an incredible relationship by utilizing words that heal.

Falling in Love – Through Your Own Love Words

Whether you have begun to look all starry-eyed years prior or hoping to become hopelessly enamored now, we can share some extremely sentimental approaches to share your emotions. Purchasing a love card or a romantic ballad is excellent; in any case, words mean more when you get them directly from your own heart. You need to realize how to state what you might want to express.

- Address it with the right "pet name"
- Use detail and don't be hesitant to get "mushy"
- Express yourself enthusiastically with love quotes
- Be inventive and unique include something new.

When writing to the love of your life, it is great to start it off with a pet name. Perhaps you have something that nobody else hears? It would be the ideal time to use it. This love letter will be among you and the one you love, so make it individual. A few people like to use (infant, sweetie, hun, and so on).

A sentimental love letter is tied to being mushy. Express yourself now with all the soft stuff that you typically don't state. Try not to keep down; after all, this is the thing that a love letter is about. Be energetic with your words, and let that individual recognize what your heart feels for them.

Presently, somewhere in the middle of the letter, use their real name. Do not overdo the pet names. It is fine to use it to start but get to their real name in the middle at least. Make sure to use love quotes all through this gem of yours. Genuine romance does not come around over and over again. Make sure to treat it well and care for it while you have it. You're telling them you love them, and with imaginative detail.

Include something new. Something you have not raised in quite a while, or at no other time. Demonstrate to them that something new emerges to you. State what your heart needed to shout the day you realized you were in love. Connections can be precarious, yet if you enable yourself to recollect how much you are in love, you will do fine.

How to Express Love Words

Communicating to a person that you genuinely like calls for the use of love words. Love is the single component that makes a society what it is. Without love, there is no life, which is why words of love are significant. There are numerous things that best display love words, and when the name is referenced, many recognize what it implies. People use multiple ways to incorporate the words. They do it orally or they write it down. The vast majority, when they were growing up, used to write love letters to one another. Today, people keep on composing love letters. It is an instrument used to display love words. It is a rare occurrence to impart these words, as it calls for certified fondness. Initially, understand that words are simply words if there is no activity to coordinate them. It is likely the best thing about love. Love is best shown when words are included. It affirms what there is in this emotional state.

In this manner, if you wish to use the words, you must reexamine yourself and see if you love the person. Sentimental love between a man and a woman is portrayed above, and a portion of the words you will discover incorporate the following: dear sweetheart, nectar, my love, my favorite, and the list go on. Love is dynamic, and people are inventive.

New ages keep on concocting love words like baby, boo, and numerous others. When it comes to utilizing these words, you must ensure that the person you are communicating with gets it. When there is viable correspondence, you can anticipate a boost in your relationship. There are vast numbers of love words you can use, and different societies and even religions may decide on these words. Different dialects will have their one-of-a-kind arrangement of love words. While you wish to express your love to somebody, it doesn't need to be sexual love. You can show respect for your children, guardians, siblings, etc. It is extremely vital to express appreciation to such people, and many do it consistently.

For example, the words people use to demonstrate love for their children include pumpkin, bear, love bear, daylight, baby, and the list goes on. Think of your one-of-a-kind words, which can be a nickname as long as it is equipped with love. It is important to be active in showing love to other people. In society, some people frequently feel dismissed. Such people might not have dear companions or family. Life is desolate when you have nobody to impart your love to, and you ought to endeavor to express love any place and whenever conceivable.

If you're the sort of person who isn't active in showing love, begin doing it, and you don't need to write a love letter. It is simply how you state it. Love can include numerous viewpoints so figure out how to radiate your emotions through your relationships.

Using Words of Love to Inspire the Relationship – 3 Tips for Men to Learn

Relationships are a back and forth movement in the life of many of us as we clear our path through the riddles of life and of love. To live in the steady fight is to live in the bogus acknowledgment that one way or another, there are always victors and failures as we cross the minefield of love.

We come at it from an altogether different points of view, especially as we take a gander at the words we use to get us to where we even have a relationship. Men, generally, need a considerable amount of assistance in this field and typically avoid love words because of poor role models, societal impacts, peer pressure.

There is always a way out, yet numerous men neglect to search for a way to talk about love to their partners. So, just what are a few ways to make words mean something to your partner? A couple of tips always prove to useful, right men?

Tip 1:

Women need to hear your heart. It is most likely one of the hardest things for men to do as it is a reality to which most were never introduced. Begin small here, folks — a simple note left before work can be an incredible beginning. The significant thing is to share your heart NOW, even if you disclose to her that you are just learning.

Tip 2:

Not each cherishing word should lead to sex! Because you state something erotic doesn't imply that the spoken words are S-E-X! Get over yourself. In some cases, the most sentimental things we do will never lead to sex, nor should they.

Tip 3:

Love to love. Reevaluate your relationship as a way to love by simply cherishing your partner. If you center around your quintessence as a team, the relationship will rule your faculties.

Keep in mind, men. You are more than what you at any point. Remember that you can do great things with your words. Start now and at last, love is all there is, so let your words be your beginning.

Chapter 14:
How to Make Your Partner Feel Appreciated

One of the ways of deepening your affections for each other is through appreciating one another. Appreciation is not tied to grand actions and expensive items, but it is an expression of indebtedness and a credit to your partner's significance. The following are some of the ways you may appreciate your partner:

• **Give them compliments**. Whether it's their looks, smell, or brains, people love receiving compliments, especially when these compliments come from loved ones. There are many opportunities for complimenting your partner. Ensure that you are taking up challenges, and compliment your partner for every milestone they reach.

• **Say "Thank you" a lot more**. The funniest thing about human relationships is that we take for granted those we have "locked down." We almost become blind to the crucial role they play in our lives. So, get into the habit of thanking your partner for every little favor or task they complete for you. It doesn't matter if it's a simple favor like bringing you water or something as complex as buying you a Ferrari.

• **Don't belittle their efforts**. If they have a romantic bone in their body, your spouse will try to impress you repeatedly and somehow fail at it. For instance, they might try to prepare your favorite dish on your special day and end up ruining the kitchen or doing a lousy job of it. Be happy that they thought about you and resist criticizing their incompetence.

• **Accept them**. Always be accommodating. Nothing spurs feelings of rejection more than a spouse who won't make time for their partner. You would think that this person works in a company that's changing the world, but no, they are a mere employee doing random stuff in a forgettable company, but you wonder what they do with their time in any case. Is it social media? Ensure that you don't turn away when your significant other attempts to contact you.

• **Show them support**. Give support to your spouse as they pursue their dreams. There are more people than you'd care to know that would be happy to see your spouse failed. You want to be the opposite force. If your spouse is a talented golfer, show up at his games, and yell out his name as he swings. Spousal support gives one a rare kind of satisfaction. You know someone dependable has got your back. It makes you fearless.

• **Give them space**. Successful marriages are about giving one another area. If your presence is suffocating, your partner will soon lose respect for you, and that's how conflicts in a marriage begin. So, ensure that you are giving your partner space.

• **Make them your priority**. Let your spouse see that you care about them. Make it easy for them to get by. The biggest resource you can spend on your significant other is your time. When you give your time, you don't get it back. Thus, your spouse will greatly appreciate the fact that they are your priority. This will make them return the favor, and you will have a healthy relationship in your hands.

• **Hugs and kisses**. You can't go wrong with a tight, long hug or a light, lingering kiss on the lips. Rain on your spouse with kisses and hugs. When you are leaving and when you are coming back, seal those moments with kisses and hugs. It will make your spouse think about you a lot more.

• **Listen attentively**. When your spouse approaches you in the living room while speaking, mute the TV. Turn to them and fix your eyes on theirs. Have open body language. Nod as they talk. Show that you are keenly following their every word. It ensures that you get their intended message. You'll be in a position to fulfill the wishes of your spouse.

• **Communicate throughout the day**. Should you text-bomb him throughout the day? By no means! Just keep in touch as you tell him you're great and find out whether he's great too. Also, this is the time to build up sexual tension. Don't be afraid to tell him the naughty thought in your mind and what you plan on doing to him in the bedroom. So, later in the night, they'll be squealing like a stuck pig from ecstasy.

• **Trust your spouse**. If he wants to know something, reveal it to him in a heartbeat. Let him see that you don't second guess him. When partners trust each other, it becomes a hell of a lot more comfortable to navigate the waters of marriage. But when there's no trust, little pops up, each of them thinking that they are smarter than the other, but sooner or later, they all go down in flames.

• **Be full of surprises**. Let your partner come home Friday evening looking forward to a quiet weekend, except he enters the house and finds his bags packed with you at the side with a big smile and tickets to a Caribbean island. Of course it must be within your financial reach. Surprises don't necessarily have to be pricey. You can prepare him his favorite dish. Or buy him a new shirt.

• **Be proud of your partner**. Never be ashamed of being seen with your partner. On the contrary, show him off to the world. Introduce him to your friends as your loved one. Even your walking style should have a touch of class when he's around.

• **Be a little jealous**. When you hear guys saying they hate jealousy in a woman, they really refer to an obsession. You don't want to be obsessed with him. But you want to give him that look that says, "I'm watching you." You see a chick flirting with him; you wait until they are done, but some other time you walk up to him and go, "

Who's that chick?"

"She's so and so."

"Okay."

It shows him that you hope he won't make a decision that ruins what both of you have.

• **Forgive him**. He's no angel. Sometimes he'll make mistakes. But if he apologizes sincerely, you have got to forgive your partner.

• **Things that Your Husband Wants but Won't Say.** Relationship dynamics tend to be more complicated than one can imagine. Not everything is as it appears. Communication helps in satisfying important emotional and physical needs, but there's more room left for improvement. These are some of the things that men want from their wives, but they don't always ask for them.

• **Don't try to change him.** Most women have a mental image of their ideal man. But for some odd reason, they tend to try to hammer the man in their life to match their mental image. They ignore the fact that this man's behaviors and attitudes result from genetics and the environment, which you can't win against. If a woman deemed a man good enough to be her husband, she should overlook his faults. Men hardly transform unless they go through a particularly bad or delightful experience.

• **Physical touch**. Men want to feel their wives run their soft little hands all over their skin. They want their women to throw them in bed and straddle them and do nothing else besides run their hands over their bodies. This makes the man feel relaxed and at the same time dominated by some fierce female energy. It's incredibly arousing. While in the living room as they lie on the couch watching TV, men want their woman to come up, lie beside them and start running their sweet little hands along their thigh, occasionally stopping to squeeze it a little. They also want women to put their hands on the small of their back and rub them gently.

• **Initiate sex**. More often than not, it is the man who initiates sex. That's what most couples are used to. But who says women cannot start sex? Female hyenas dominate their males while having sex, and it appears very stimulating. Some men want a woman who takes matters into her own hands and initiates sex, and then goes ahead to pleasure like there's no tomorrow.

• **Join him in his hobby**. Men also want their women to follow them in their pursuits. One thing that makes a person mentally healthy has a hobby they can indulge in when they are free. But what would make a hobby even more pleasant? The wife coming along! Some men would like to have their wives join in on the fun, even if they don't participate. If he enjoys bowling, the wife may come along and bowl with him, or she may just cheer him on. Such tendencies will strengthen the bond between couples.

• **Become both his partner and best friend**. It is the classic case of controlled codependency. For more reasons than one, absolute codependency is dangerous for a marriage because it results in emotional exhaustion. But then you can have your wife act as your best friend too. You'll be disclosing your dirty little secrets to her. It will make your marriage even more robust. But this works well when you have other friends on the side. Men who want their wives to act like their best friends tend to desire an intense emotional connection. You will find that they can shed tears just thinking about – or looking at pictures of – their loved ones.

• **Be patient with them**. A wife can make you move at a speed that you are uncomfortable with. They can be pretty hectic to handle. Some men wish that their wives were a little more patient with them. For instance, when a man promises, he doesn't have to be reminded of that every day. It would be far more superior if the woman just lets the man fulfill his promises when he's ready. When you are patient with your man, you give him ample time to gain focus and establish important things in his life.

• **Be on his side**. Life can be challenging. You are never guaranteed success. Things could be going well today, but tomorrow, everything could be in a state of disarray. To survive in this big green jungle known as planet earth, you need strong-willed people at your side. Men wish that their wives would become their strongest supporters. In this modern era where both men and women have careers to worry about, it can be pretty hard to meet a woman who's into "nurturing" her man. But still, it doesn't stop some men from wishing that their wives were demonstrably their number one fans.

• **Don't criticize their weaknesses**. Most of the time, men are held to impossibly high standards, and there's pressure coming from every side they turn to. When a man who appears to be beneath these standards comes along, they find themselves getting made fun of.

Nothing breaks a man more than having his ego shattered. Thus, a man appreciates a wife cut from a different cloth than the world. Such a wife shouldn't mind that he doesn't make six figures yet. Instead, helps him look for ways to maximize his earnings. Instead of making him feel small, the wife should appreciate his efforts and always look to the bright side. Such positivity allows him to tap into his creative energy and develop a concept that will scale his wealth.

Chapter 15:
Practical Communication Skills in Relationships

Communication is the basis for a healthy and balanced marriage. It's just how you and also your spouse link, share your thoughts and views and settle disagreements. Relationship interaction abilities do not come simply for everybody. Some pairs will undoubtedly need to work with their techniques for several years. But gradually, they are able to talk honestly and truthfully with one another. No matter just how connected you and your partner are currently, there is constantly space to reinforce and grow your partnership.

Eye Contact

Preserving eye contact is both excellent methods of teaching your partner you are listening. Whether your partner is telling a joke or revealing a deep family key, give them your full attention. Put away disruptive technology, mute or turn off the TV, and lean in towards your companion. This will undoubtedly show you care about their info. You can make a spot in your home where the electronic devices can be positioned to limit technical diversions.

Don't Disrupt Your Partner

Being interrupted is the quickest means to escalate a debate. When interacting with your partner, it's essential that both people feel they have a chance to speak and be listened to. It may contact tempting to squeeze in your very own viewpoint while your partner is still talking, specifically if you feel they have a fact incorrect, yet it is necessary to wait. Offering your companion your focus while remaining focused and attached programs your partner regard.

Develop a Neutral Area

Communicating isn't always straightforward. Lots of pairs locate it beneficial to tackle "hard" martial subjects in a neutral zone, such as the cooking area table. It may sound silly, yet assessing your partner's lack of sex-related expertise while in bed can make them feel attacked and also can cause them to view the room in an adverse light in the future. Saying at a loved one's house is another instance of one partner sensation like they have the typical "high ground" in the argument.

Talk in Person

Among the best communication abilities in relationships, you can use always mentioning vital topics one-on-one. Texting is certainly not the avenue for having significant relationship discussions or for making big choices since the tone of voice cannot be figured out with text messages. Instead, pick a time when you can be one-on-one with your companion.

Use "I" Declarations When Problems Arise

One issue pairs face when they are arguing is assaulting each other. By using "I" statements, you take the stress off your partner. Rather than stating, "YOU did this, and it made me angry," attempt interacting with, "I feel that when THIS took place, my feelings were injured." See the difference? You made the issue your very own, as opposed to striking your companion. This easy yet effective strategy protects against either of you from going into attack mode or coming to be unnecessarily protective with each other.

Be Straightforward with Your Partner

Being truthful isn't always easy, yet it is crucial to a healthy and balanced relationship. One study about "12 Healthy and Balanced Dating Partnership High qualities" found that excellent communication, sincerity, as well as a trust fund were noted as several of the best quality. Being honest means informing your partner when you feel some issues require to be talked about. It likewise indicates confessing when you were wrong and also asking forgiveness as opposed to making justifications. Not just does sincerity assistance promote real open interaction between you as well as your partner, it also helps construct depend on.

Discuss the Little Points

Among the excellent communication abilities in re-enforcing connections is when you, as well as your partner, can speak about the low points in addition to the big things. You can strengthen your marriage by discussing your day, your ideas, or sharing amusing stories from your week. When you are wed, every subject ought to be open for discussion. There should not be anything that is as well as uncomfortable or uncomfortable to share. By talking about the little things, you will undoubtedly make it much easier to speak about more important topics in the future.

Utilize the 24-Hour-Rule

When two individuals are married and living together, there are bound to be bumps in the roadway. Some days you are most likely to seem like rainbows and butterflies drift through your house when your companion is near. Other times, you'll feel a frustration beginning when your partner is close. If you are feeling disappointed with your companion as well as are about to articulate your grievance, pause for a moment. Practice the 24-hour guideline. So, she didn't empty the dishwashing machine, or he did not pick up his socks. Is it truly the completion of the globe? Will it matter to you in 24-hours? Otherwise, take into consideration letting it go.

Make a Physical Call

No matter what tone your discussion is taking, physical contact is significant. Low-intensity excitement of the skin, such as touching a companion or brushing their arm, promotes the release of oxytocin. The love hormone promotes bonding as well as empathy in charming companions, and it also works as an anti-stress representative as well as advertises cooperative behavior.

Make Communication Fun

Interacting is just how you talk about household as well as economic issues, problems and their options, and how you and also your partner choose. However, do not fail to remember that interaction needs to be enjoyable, as well. Chatting with your companion indicates sharing funny tales and dreams for the future, as well as cooperating in deep conversation. These are the moments that produce a more profound emotional link and increase oxytocin as well as dopamine. Always make time to sign in with your spouse vocally, whether the discussion that adheres to is significant or foolish.

Chapter 16:
Developing Trust

Trust is an important element in any wholesome relationship. When your relationship is lacking in trust, it is hard getting close to your partner and depend on them for any form of support. It follows that you cannot truly love with no trust.

This means that we can only truly love someone we have faith in. After all, trust is earned through displayed behavior. It remains the feeling of safety that allows all parties in a relationship to bare themselves fully, devoid of any fear or judgment.

And if someone breaks your faith by any means, shape, or method, then what you feel is not true love. Hence, building trust is essential even before marriage, but marriage should ensure that this trust grows with time.

Tips for Cultivating Trust in Your Marriage

You stand as human, not a supernatural being, but you can still do your utmost to meet certain hopes of your partner. And among these expectations that require fulfillment is fidelity. Within this area, for instance, you can stay devoted to your partner if you really agree on making your marriage work. After all, if you tied the knot with that person, and at that point, you were actually committed to the relationship.

1. Live as if each day is your final day. Once you keep this in mind, you will live ready to die and set for God's judgment. This attitude will assist in controlling yourself when facing temptations.

Additionally, it will hinder you from playing with fire and stay away from whatever does not belong to you, be it things or people.

2. Remember your marriage promises every day and remain loyal to them. Considering that it was your sole decision to tie the knot with your spouse, then he/she must be the right one for you and no one else. So, although you may admire other people, no one can surpass the level of admiration you have for your spouse. Moreover, you must synchronize your actions to your words, especially in terms of your marriage vows.

3. Aside from your marriage vows, keep all your promises. Once you promise something to your other half, keep it. This will strengthen the trust of your spouse in you, as well as making you more credible. Your other half will certainly adore your reliability, besides not having second thoughts whenever you make promises to her/him.

4. Only make responsible promises. Before making a vow to your better half, ensure first your ability to satisfy that promise. Thus, you must thoughtfully consider whatever you will for your partner. Never rush in making promises just to appease your spouse because the test is in delivering that promise you made.

5. Show honesty at all times. Truthfulness is the good quality of a person that we all want to seek when building trust in marriage. It must be our perpetual aim to boost the routine of absolute precision in all communications with our better half. After all, lies abolish trust in all marriages.

6. Admit wrongdoings and apologize to your spouse. Indeed, it sometimes hurts when you admit your wrongdoings. Moreover, it is never easy to muster the courage to do this, but this is also a way of showing honesty. Even when your spouse may not be happy with what you did, they will learn to admire you for doing this.

7. Be fully sincere with your partner. Keeping secrets from your spouse can cause distrust in your marriage. Sometimes, our pride and ego hinder fully opening ourselves to our spouses. To prevent this from happening, try involving your partner in all the choices you make.

8. Never bring about the occasion wherein your spouse would feel that they are very nosy. For example, when you are leaving home, and your partner asks where you are going, you should tell precisely where you plan to go with details. In the first place, you should always tell your spouse where you are so as not to worry about you needlessly. This can also nip the chances of your spouse doubting you in the bud.

9. Give your spouse timely information. When you get home late, it is natural for your spouse to want to know the reason for this. So, even when you feel so tired and annoyed by being questioned, be patient to provide them with the info immediately to build trust in your marriage. In this case, it would have been best if you had informed your spouse before leaving home that day or called him ahead of time to prevent being questioned when you got home.

10. Try pleasing your spouse whenever possible. When you thoroughly try to make your spouse happy, it makes them feel that they can completely depend on you with nothing to fear or doubt. Learn to possess the attitude that says, "I accept that I cannot get all my desires and needs fulfilled within this marriage; however, I will accomplish to my best capacity, expressing affection and trying to meet my spouse's needs. Thus, I will share, give, and bear." Your partner will have faith in you because you stay committed to your marriage.

11. Forgive yourself and your spouse. You can develop trust again within your marriage when you forgive them from the bottom of your heart. Reconciliation results from forgiveness, which paves the means for you to clear the pain from your thoughts and let it go.

12. Practice humility. When you have wronged your partner, apologize and request forgiveness. Admit your wrongdoing, express how terribly you felt about whatever you did towards your spouse, the way you have reflected about it several times over, what lessons you learned from that experience, and the manner you plan to modify your behavior onward.

When you have shown by your conduct that you remain remorseful, your spouse will see the transformation in your outlook. Always reminding yourself of the loss of whatever you did will serve as a tool to avoid making the same mistake.

Trust-Building Exercises. The cornerstone of any lasting relationship is trust. Apart from communication, trust is one of the most important things you must concentrate on. Building trust certainly takes some time and re-establishing it will take some effort too. You are two different people with different personalities, experiences, and perspectives about the world as well as your lives. So, trust is not only important to forge a bond with each other but it also helps you stay together in the long run. A relationship devoid of trust will not last. When mutual trust exists, it shows you and your partner are completely safe in the relationship. Also, the lack of trust is a common reason why a lot of relationships never last. Trust forms the basis for emotional intimacy and a real connection. Therefore, maintaining trust in your relationship is quintessential. Couple's counseling is a great way to build trust. However, if you do not have the time or access to a couple's counselor, how do you work on this? Do not you worry because I have your back here! If you want to build more trust in your relationship, here are a couple of trust-building exercises you can try as a couple.

Your Phones. A common source of trust issues encompassed these days seems to be technology and social media-based. Be open about the phone as well as social media, as this is a great way for a couple to build trust in the relationship. This is a very important area to work on, especially if a couple is dealing with any infidelity issues. At times, it might be quite difficult to rely on someone else's words solely.

Instead, if you can look at tangible evidence, like a phone, as it helps rebuild trust. Decide upon an activity you are both comfortable with related to your smartphones or social media and take it from there. I am not suggesting that you keep checking your partner's phone, but it does help establish a certain degree of trust when you do not hide your phone from your partner. For instance, when you are talking to your partner and keep ignoring a phone call or avoid replying to any messages, it leads to unnecessary mistrust. Be honest and open about who you talk to and converse with. For the sake of the health of your relationship, work on building some trust.

Plan Date Nights. One of the most important aspects of having some trust in a relationship is to give up a little control. We all want to control because it gives you a sense of security. When you know you are the one doing everything, you have complete control. Every decision you make is yours, and you are not relying on anyone else. However, if you do not give up a little control once in a while in the relationship, your partner might start resenting you. Do not be controlling, and do not micromanage. For a relationship to survive, you and your partner must both do your bit. One person cannot keep making all the effort while the other does nothing. Another simple way to give up a level of control is to take turns planning your weekly date nights.

Couple Activities. Whenever you try something new, you are essentially stepping out of your comfort zone. This is a great way not just to form a stronger bond but also to build trust. An engaging way to build trust is by indulging in a new activity like dancing. Any activity that requires you to pair with someone else and involves a degree of coordination and synchronization will be helpful. Since you essentially depend on your partner to perfect a pose or a movement, it creates a sense of mutual trust. This is also a fun way to establish trust. Apart from this, it is entertaining and fun too! You will not only end up having fun together but also get an opportunity to learn a new skill.

Vision Board. A simple activity you and your partner can do together is to create a vision board. A vision board consists of your relationship goals and what you want your relationship to be like. Go through various magazines and come up with images or phrases you can use to describe what you want your future to look like. You can easily determine the aspects you want more and less of. This is a simple activity that allows you to start a discussion about your future together. Having "the talk" is never easy, and this is a fun way to go about doing it. You can also make a date night out of this activity.

Your Fears. When you make yourself vulnerable and share your fears with a partner, the interest in your relationship will deepen. Showing your vulnerability enables you to address any fears you both have, along with any insecurity. While doing this, ensure that neither you nor your partner is being judgmental or critical of what the other person says. Do not be scared of being judged. Talking about your worries, fears, or insecurities does not make you weak. It only makes you human.

In fact, it might give your partner a chance to understand you and your behaviors fully. Likewise, it will give you an insight into your partner's feelings, emotions, and behaviors. Once everything is out in the open, it becomes easier to address any underlying causes of any trust issues in your relationship.

Chapter 17:
Setting Relationship Goals

Make it a point to set goals about communication, love, compromise, commitment, sexual intimacy, household chores, and support. These are the main aspects that influence the quality and strength of a relationship. Once you cover these areas and come up with attainable goals, you can improve your relationship.

It is quintessential that you and your partner both work on improving the way you communicate. While setting goals in this area, think about ways in which you can improve your communication.

Take some time, sit down with your partner, and asked them what they need. Emotional support is not the only form of support you can provide your partner with. At times, something as simple as driving your partner to the grocery store or taking them to the dentist are forms of support too.

For a relationship to last, there needs to be friendship in it. You must be more than just partners; you must be friends first. Come up with different things you and your partner can do together. Shared activity certainly helps increase your degree of closeness. You and your partner can also take turns selecting different activities you can try out together.

I am certain you love your partner, but how expressive are you? If you don't express your love, how will your partner ever know? How often do you express your thoughts? I'm not suggesting that you need to keep telling your partner repeatedly that you love them, but there are little things you can do which convey your love for them. For instance, sharing in on any household responsibilities, cooking their favorite meal, or hugging them as soon as you wake up in the morning are all ways to show your love. In a long-term relationship, it is quintessential that you express your love and affection for your partner.

A relationship will not last if there are no compromises. My way or the highway kind of thinking can quickly shatter any relationship. Instead, learn to compromise. It is okay if you don't always get your way, and it is okay if you are not always right. Start making an effort to understand your partner's perspective. Learn to negotiate and understand the importance of coming to compromises. When you compromise, it doesn't mean that you are wrong while your partner is right; it merely means that you love your partner more and are willing to concentrate on the relationship instead of any other petty issues or problems.

So, make a conscious effort and set certain goals for physical intimacy in your relationship. Be a responsive and caring lover to your partner. Spend some time to discuss with your partner all the various things you want to try and be open with them. Learn to cater to not just your needs but the needs of your partner as well.

A common problem a lot of couples run into is related to household responsibilities. I believe in the equality of partners, and therefore partners must share all responsibilities. After all, you are living together, so why not share the responsibilities? Spend some time and come up with a schedule to divide responsibilities between the two of you so that one partner doesn't always feel burdened with household work. This is quintessential, especially if you and your partner have day jobs to attend to as well.

Tips to Keep in Mind

Happiness doesn't always come from getting what you want, but it can come from moving toward what you desire. When it comes to relationships, it essentially means that couples must have a couple of goals they are moving toward together. So, how can couples support and motivate each other to achieve their individual goals along with the relationship goals? How to reach your goals while maintaining your relationship's health.

The first step is to ensure that your individual goals are in perfect alignment with your relationship goals. This alignment is quintessential to create a sense of harmony, which allows you both to attain your personal goals. Once this harmony is present, there is no limit to the things you can achieve as a team.

It is time to make two plans - a six-month plan and a two-year plan. Think of these as short and long-term goals for your relationship. Discuss what you plan on doing, where you want to be, and how you want to be within these two timeframes. The next step is to visualize and think about where you want your life to be in the next five, 10, 15, and 20 years. Don't judge your partner, and don't allow your partner to judge you. Keep an open mind toward each other and attentively listen to what the other person has to say.

Spend some time and make a list of all your personal goals. You and your partner must do this individually and then spend some time together to discuss the lists you both made. Include short-term as well as long-term goals and discuss this if you feel like you're getting stuck while making this list.

Whenever you are setting any goals, the goals must be such that they make you feel good about yourself. If the goal you are setting for yourself or your relationship goes against everything you believe in, you will not be able to achieve it. The goals you set for yourself must not only be good for you but must be good for your relationship as well. When you have shared goals, it not only becomes easier to achieve them, but the health of your relationship also improves along the way.

Regardless of the goal you set, make sure that the goals are specific, realistic, and attainable. If a goal doesn't fulfill even one of these conditions, you are merely setting yourself up for failure. People often think that setting lofty goals for themselves is a good idea. They seem to stand by the age-old adage of, "If you shoot for the stars, you will land on the moon." Well, I don't think this is the right way to go about setting goals. After all, if you don't attain your goals, it will be a source of massive disappointment and discontent. To avoid this, ensure that the goals you are setting are realistic, attainable, and quite specific.

You and your partner must come up with an arrangement that helps you stay focused and accountable for any commitments you make. The relationship you share with your partner is quite sacred, and you must cherish and nourish it. The arrangements you create must support you and your partner along with your relationship. It's not about getting rewards or punishments to create accountability. It is about coming up with a mutually beneficial plan to create accountability for each other.

It is okay to concentrate on your goals, but it is not okay to overlook any victories you attain along the way. Attaining your goals is seldom a sprint and is always a marathon. So, the journey to your goals matters as much as the goal itself. You and your partner must be appreciative of each other and each other's accomplishments. Rejoice in all the small wins in your lives. Celebrate each other's successes. By doing this, you are naturally cementing the bond you share. If you celebrate every milestone you cross, it will give you the motivation to keep going.

You must be supportive and understanding. Support and encourage your partner to achieve their goals, and your partner will reciprocate these gestures. Give your partner the room they need to attain their goals and don't become a hurdle. Keep a conscious check on any criticism you dole out. If your partner is making a mistake, feel free to correct them, but do so gently.

Be each other's support system. In such instances, be each other's cheerleaders. Your relationship will be happy and more satisfactory when you know you have your partner's support, and the same applies to your partner. Make it a point to seek feedback from your partner to see how they are doing. By asking for their feedback, you are making them feel important and giving yourself a chance to view things from a fresh perspective.

Spend some time and make a note of all your goals. Keep reviewing these goals as you go about your daily life. Your goals can change, or the way you want to achieve them might change. You might also need to tweak your goals occasionally. So, don't forget to include a weekly review session of your goals.

The final step is quite simple - always remember that you are a team. Achieving goals becomes easier when you are doing it together. You don't have to do everything by yourself, and you can count on your partner for additional help or support. Once you have accomplished your dreams or goals, don't forget to come up with new goals.

Chapter 18:
Significant Habits of
Good Relationships

Habits have a significant effect on any relationship. When it comes to having a good relationship, there are certain behaviors that can have a strong and positive impact. It's essential to be aware when forming routines, especially for your relationship.

Significant Habits of Good Relationships

You need to make an effort every single day to perform good habits, so they become part of the routine to you.

Always show respect

Showing respect for your partner is a habit worth making, and it is an ingredient necessary to create a happy, safe, and long-lasting relationship. You express your affection, appreciation, and comfort when you show respect for your partner. If you show contempt, you convey that your spouse is not acknowledged. Respecting your partner, despite variations, is all about valuing them for who they are. You may have another view on life, but that doesn't mean you can neglect and put down your friend.

If experiencing conflicts, make sure you respect the disagreements between your spouses. This does not allow you to offend your partner in front of friends and family or in public. Also, show respect, especially when you're in disagreement.

Go for a stroll with your friend/partner

This is a ritual formed by a husband and where they find a deeper connection in their relationship. If you love nature and spend time with your mate, make it a habit to walk— either in the mornings before beginning your day or at night. For example, husband and wife can walk on Sunday mornings and in the evenings. It's a mental decision they make to go out together every day. It encourages communication, fresh air access, and quality time.

Once you develop this routine, the body may actually want to go out. It is noticed with couples when they made it a habit to walk at night and on Sunday mornings that their bodies became ready to spend this quality time. Walking with your partner also promotes good fitness and can be as easy as walking up and down the block. Decide how long and how often you'd like to walk with your partner; the major thing is to being on the same page and make sure you make the mental decision to build this routine together.

In the night time turn off the television and be with your friend. How can you relate to your partner when there's always television? There is no bond established when you both look at the television screen endlessly in the evenings. Take the mental decision to turn off the television at night and spend time together in quality. You may be able to snuggle and watch a movie sometimes but avoid watching TV most evenings.

Take the time to chat with your friend about their day and how they're doing. This behavior causes love and attachment. Snuggle up and chat on the sofa with your partner; talk to each other and what you two can do to strengthen your relationship. Whether it's preparing for the next holiday or your next date night, there will always be something to consider. Focus on developing your relationship and discuss issues you need to tackle.

In the morning, take some tea with your partner. This simple gesture indicates a great deal to my husband. He loves drinking coffee and it shows morning love and affection to get it to him. If your partner likes to drink tea in the morning, through this act of personal service, create that habit and express love. When you bring a cup of tea to him, it shows you care. this is one great way you can show love to him. Wake up a few minutes earlier so you can spend some quality time together with your partner before going to work. This is an easy yet powerful habit of happy relationships.

Share positive attributes about your partner with others

The habit of sharing positive attributes about your partner can help the relationship deepen. Alternatively, sharing negative attributes about your partner will only build a tall wall between the two of you. Do you know a couple who always argue with friends in public and show negative characteristics about each other? This is a bad habit that inevitably wrecks any friendship. This destructive behavioral pattern causes distrust, disconnection, and disrespect. Get used to projecting positive attributes for others. An optimistic behavioral trend produces respect, appreciation, and devotion.

Suggestion: take the life-potential evaluation of Lifehack and get a personalized report based on your unique strengths. Find out how to start living your entire life and achieve your full potential.

Reconnect throughout the day

We have such busy routines that it can be the last priority to communicate with your partner throughout the day, but if you want a healthy, long-lasting relationship, reconnecting-connecting-connecting with your partner throughout the day is important. It is as easy as sending a romantic text or calling your partner on the way home or during your lunch break. This habit is meant to keep your partner linked and focused. You can still take the time to send a text message or make a phone call, even if you have a hectic schedule. Render yourself artistic. Think of ways you can reconnect-connected-connect with your partner all day.

Take time to think

Take time to think about what makes you feel loved the most and how your partner feels the most affection by looking at these five love languages. Imagine having a tank of love inside of you. Your love tank is filled up each time your partner speaks your love language. Your love tank runs low each time your partner doesn't convey your love language. When it comes to important behaviors of happy relationships, establishing the habit of speaking the love language of your partner on a daily basis creates in your relationship passion, affection, and warmth.

Cooking and cleaning

Cooking with your partner is always much more fun. I know when John helps me; I enjoy cooking a lot more. Cooking together builds intimacy, communication, and love; creating and eating food when you are with your partner becomes an intimate act. I express my love by cooking and eating with my husband (with the TV off), which creates a deeper bond between us. This is a big opportunity to spend time together in quality.

If you prefer cooking or your partner, make it a habit that the other person cleans. John and I have a habit of cleaning up afterward whenever I cook, and vice versa. It shows appreciation for my cooking when John cleans after I cook and that he values me. It is important that you always love and respect your spouse, even if the cleaning of the dishes is as easy as that. It's nice to know John appreciates the love I put into my cooking, and it's a sign of love-affection to want to do the dishes. Become mentally stronger!

Become Stronger

Every day show love for your partner and welcome to your partner! It is just as simple as this. Whatever love you want to show in your relationship, do it. Do this on a single day. It's about showing your gratitude to your partner when it comes to important traditions of happy relationships. This can be leaving a love note at the end of the day before going to work or taking flowers home. It goes back to the love language of your mate. Find the language of love for your partner and show your gratitude through their language of love.

If your partner feels valued by the quality of time, make sure to "turn off" and focus your attention on your partner when you get back home from work. Sit down on the couch and be with your partner. Whichever language your partner loves, make sure you speak the same language. Make it a habit of showing your partner appreciation every single day.

Working together as a team towards objectives (short-and long-term) A happy relationship focuses on short-and long-term objectives. Unhappy couples have nothing in their lives to look forward to. Focus on creating, establishing, and attaining goals within your relationship. Happy couples have ambitions, small as well as large. Follow this template setting target and start cultivating your partner link.

Spend quality time

In the morning, be with a partner before beginning the day. Surely this practice starts to enhance your relationship and the bond you have together. We have such hectic schedules that it is even more important to take the time to talk with your partner in the mornings. Reflect and understand what had brought you two together. It's easy to allow tension, anger, and distractions to get in the way of a happy relationship, but when you take time in the morning to love and appreciate your partner, you're building a routine filled with comfort, affection, and care.

Conclusion

Keeping things bottled up can lead to problems in the relationship itself, and you should always be able to express yourself. This last guide will summarize what you have learned in so you can be a more successful couple. If you have a strong relationship, then you're on your way to success.

A relationship is a dynamic process that involves interactions of people who have developed an interdependent relationship with one another. In order to develop this interdependency, psychological mechanisms have evolved that are programmed into our brain and become activated as soon as we enter into an intimate relationship. These mechanisms affect our emotional well-being and dictate how we react to our partners in any given situation. The main purpose of these mechanisms is to make sure that humans bond together intimately and raise children successfully in order to preserve the human species.

You should always try to understand each other's point of view. It is essential, and you should always be open-minded and willing to listen to what your partner has to say. Both of you need to know what the other person wants out of the relationship, which will help improve your communication if you both understand each other.

You must communicate with each other for things to go well in your relationship. When communication is going well, it will lead to a stronger bond. If you understand each other's feelings, then you'll be able to have many conversations with each other.

It's also important for both of you to understand the other person's needs. If you don't understand your partner's needs, they will become frustrated and become angry with you over little things.

You should always try to have conflict resolution discussions with your partner. You need to resolve things quickly to avoid conflict, which doesn't have to happen simultaneously. Conflict is very common, but you should always handle a situation calmly and professionally. Being able to resolve things calmly is important because it will give both of you a good thought process and will make you a better couple overall.

Silence is not the solution for the conflict. If you're angry at your partner, you should express those feelings. Both of you need to communicate how you feel through conflict. It will help reduce the tension in the relationship, and both of you can come to a resolution that suits everyone.

You need to understand that conflict is also very common in relationships. Communication is how you resolve things in this situation, and both of you need to be able to talk about occurring problems. If you can't talk about it, you should try and work through it.

You need to try and solve problems calmly. You should always resolve issues in your relationship. Still, if you aren't going to have a conversation with your partner, you shouldn't expect that they will understand what is going on in the relationship otherwise. If you want to improve your relationship, you should have communication with each other. Communication is the way to build a close bond as a couple, and neither of you should be afraid to express your feelings.

You must always communicate with each other to make both of you happy. Communication is an essential pillar of any relationship, and both partners in the relationship need to understand and express their feelings throughout the entire process. You should always be honest with each other, and you need to speak your mind. There should not be any secrets. Honesty is the best policy.

It's important for both of you to be open-minded about the relationship. You need to understand that not everything will go perfectly, and it's okay as long as you have an open mind. You will learn from your mistakes and will have a much stronger bond because of it.

Finally, we hope this book has helped you improve your relationships and help you have a good one with your partner. Good luck with your effective communication, and we hope for good things to come to your relationship.

www.ingramcontent.com/pod-product-compliance
Lightning Source LLC
Chambersburg PA
CBHW060950050726
47592CB00003B/1185